built
for britain:
bridges
to beach
huts

Peter
Ashley

A John Wiley and Sons, Ltd, Publication

Executive Commissioning Editor: Helen Castle
Production Manager: Amie Jackowski Tibble
Project Editor: Miriam Swift
Publishing Assistant: Calver Lezama
Content Editor: Françoise Vaslin

ISBN 978-0-470-74595-3

Photo credits: All photos © Peter Ashley
Cover photo © Peter Ashley
Cover design by Parent
Page design and layouts by Anikst Design
Printed in Italy by Printer Trento

Title page: **Detail of railway footbridge,
Oakham, Rutland**

Contents

Foreword

Built for Britain is a celebration of the infectious enthusiasm that is the Betjeman in all of us; and Peter Ashley's prose, which accompanies his exquisite photography, is near poetry. The journey the book takes is entertaining, leaving behind the more learned descriptions that reduce similar books to catalogues.

Through this infectious enthusiasm, *Built for Britain* refreshes our view of old favourites such as the Forth Bridge, introduces us to modern treasures and discovers for us lost gems such as Maxim's (of machine gun fame) fairground ride in Blackpool that was in 1900 a money-spinner based on, and built to fund, a rig for testing his aircraft designs.

For anybody who wants to know more, many of the projects Peter visits are documented more formally on the website www.engineering-timelines. com, where one can not only discover the facts, but also link back into the lives of the engineers and search out similar or surrounding projects. As such, this *Built for Britain* is a sampler through which one can smell the paintwork, and complements the website where one can discover the whole meal.

Built for Britain is about restoring our sense of wonder in engineering – not a pocket guide, more for reading under the blankets with a torch.

Mark Whitby

Introduction

The unrivalled joy in photographing and writing this book has been in the discovery of structures in Britain that I had only seen at a distance, or had only been able to appreciate through other lensmen's images. Prime examples would be the sound mirrors way out on the Denge Marsh between Greatstone-on-Sea and Lydd Airport in Kent, and Sir Owen Williams's factories for Boots in Nottingham, both part of an unsung interwar heritage. I first saw the acoustic mirrors as a nine year old, grabbing my father's sleeve and pointing to their intriguing shapes glimpsed between the bungalows lining the route of our passage on the Romney, Hythe & Dymchurch Light Railway. Fifty-odd years later the thin threads of tenuous connection started to weave together. My father would have been on his annual holiday from his job toiling in a Boots dispensary, and I remember him coming back from his frequent visits to the Nottingham headquarters and showing me the company brochures. They always included monochrome photographs of Boots girls in hygienic white hats packing medicines in Williams's steel-framed building. Images of both of these structures were collected for this book in the same week of blazing May sunshine. And both of these adventures, as well as many others, were the result of precious time given up by individuals to lend me a guiding hand. I have thanked them in my acknowledgements, but I must apologise to the Boots lady, who had to gently remind me of the speed limit on the vast Nottingham complex, such was my enthusiasm for what I was about to see after all those years.

It went on. The director of the Papplewick Pumping Station not only allowed me in outside of normal visiting days, but after showing me around left me to my own devices to roam at will. I could have stayed in this hallowed hall of Victoriana for at least a week, a dishevelled author found asleep in an empty boiler, a smile of utter satisfaction on his sooty face. And then the unexpected discoveries – the once-floating coal

hopper on Goole harbour that had me standing on a wall for 20 minutes waiting first for a few weak beams of light to show it off; then, when they did, for anxious passers-by to see me shouting across the dock in an attempt to get a flock of pigeons to fly up into the air. They didn't oblige. But sun, steam and clouds combined to do all the right things for me as I stood in a field eyeing up the simply gargantuan Ratcliffe-on-Soar cooling towers.

It will be very apparent that I have enjoyed myself immeasurably in putting together this book, and I hope that it gives you as much pleasure. If one boy or girl glances up from their Nintendo to spend a few minutes looking at these wonderful presences in our landscape, and thinks they'd like to be an engineer or architect, then everyone's efforts in producing this book will have been doubly worth it.

above
**The hot shingle walk,
Greatstone-on-Sea,
Kent**

industry

above
**Papplewick Pumping
Station from across the
Cooling Pond**

opposite
**Beam engines,
decorative fish and
stained-glass water lily**

opposite far right
**Mahogany- and brass-
clad engine cylinder**

Papplewick is a cathedral of waterworks. A red brick
pumping station and tall chimney stand amongst the
dark green of pines and shrubberies, looking out over
a serene cooling pond that appears more ornamental
lake than utility. Inside the engine house two Watt &
Co beam engines, resplendent in red and gold livery,
each used about six tons of coal a day in order for an
engine to pump 6.8 million litres (1.5 million gallons)
of clean, fresh water southwards to the rapidly
expanding population of industrial Nottingham.

The visionary engineer was Marriott Ogle
Tarbotton, who followed Thomas Hawksley's 1879–80
Papplewick Reservoir with his supervision of the
Pumping Station in the early 1880s. Originally there
were to be two engine houses, the absence of the

second resulting in the curious offsetting of what was intended to be a central chimney. Inside is a Temple of Water with three-dimensional gold fishes swimming through wrought-iron reeds on cast-iron columns, windows blossoming with stained-glass water lilies. Once only experienced by the workers and members of the Board, but now a treat for everybody as the beam engines pound into life again on special steam days.

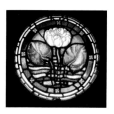

13

Abbey Mills Pumping Station, West Ham, London

above
Abbey Mills Pumping Station in West Ham

opposite
The spectacular central cupola

'Cleanliness is next to godliness'. That's the kind of motto the Victorians embroidered on their hearts; the sort of thing you'd expect to see run out in ceramic tiling at swimming baths. Sir Joseph Bazalgette would certainly have taken the sentiment on board when he first conceived these imposing works – one of the pumping stations for dealing with the effluent flowing eastwards from his new London sewers. Architect Charles Driver's 1868 Abbey Mills is the best of four structures brought on stream to do the business, as it were, of pumping sewage up into the Northern Outfall Sewer and off to the treatment works at Beckton Reach.

They describe it as 'Venetian Gothic', complete with Byzantine windows and a stunning central lantern. Inside, eight Cornish beam engines pounded away, the exhaust being carried off into the West Ham skies by two tall chimneys crowned with minaret-style cowls. These were demolished in the Second World War in case they acted as markers for German bombers homing in on the capital. The steam engines were replaced by electrically powered engines, but they still hummed away in a temple of decorative cast-iron columns and wrought-iron staircases.

Power stations dominate the flat landscape in this part of the world: Ferrybridge and Drax in Yorkshire, and in the Nottinghamshire Trent Valley at West Burton, Cottam, Ratcliffe-on-Soar and the now closed High Marnham. Turn off the M1 at junction 24 and drive towards Nottingham on the A453 and your sightline will be filled by this set of towers at Ratcliffe-on-Soar. Or at least by the cloud formations made from the rising evaporation of cooling hot water used in the generation of electricity. Commissioned here in 1968, these giant towers are known in the trade as hyperboloids, and can be 200 metres (656 feet) tall by 328 metres (1,076 feet) in diameter. Reminders of both the technological advances that swept England in the 1960s, and the apparent ease with which such environmentally dominant structures were built without much political opposition.

Here, where the River Soar decants into the Trent, are four pairs of hyperboloids cooling down one of the biggest coal-powered stations in the country. I won't

get into the whys and wherefores of this kind of electricity generation, but I do find it very pleasing that local fish love the environment and sandpipers migrate back from Africa just so that they can nest in the ash heaps.

opposite
Eight hyperboloid cooling towers at Ratcliffe-on-Soar Power Station

above
Cottam Power Station by the Trent in Nottinghamshire

above and right
Iron frame for the Oval's famous gas holder, next to The Cricketers pub, Kennington Oval

opposite top
Gas holder in the back streets of Peterborough

opposite centre
Spiral-guided holder in Bedford

opposite bottom
Iron frame for a St Pancras gas holder, London

The word 'gasometer' was first used by William Murdoch in the early 1800s, although he was describing gas *holders* for his newly invented gas for lighting, rather than a measuring device. Rearing up over the rooftops of their domestic and industrial customers, they are very familiar in the urban environment. I think as children we all expected that gas holders were bound to blow up in our faces at any minute – you only had to look at them. We see Victorian iron-framed holders on the approach to St Pancras station, and in the background of Oval cricket matches, but the spiral-guided holders, as seen here next to the Charles Wells Brewery in Bedford and in Peterborough, are now the most ubiquitous.

Still constructed up to 1983, large gas holders will each typically hold up to 35,000 cubic metres (1.2 million cubic feet) of gas in 60-metre- (196-foot-) diameter drums. These days they move up and down, not so much as gas is used (teatime every day sees them start to lower), but more as a device to maintain correctly balanced pressure in the system of gas pipes. Another, unsung, use for gas holders was as markers on the approach to airports. At Southall 'LH' for Heathrow was painted on the circular roof of one, at South Harrow 'NO' for RAF Northolt. Had this negative word been there in 1960 it might have prevented a Pan Am Boeing 707 landing here instead of at Heathrow.

Wakerley Lime Kilns, Northamptonshire

Way out of its normal habitat, the London & North Western Railway (LNWR) once ran alongside the willow-fringed banks of the Welland between Market Harborough and Wakerley, before leaving the river to wind across to Peterborough. Here, between the village and Barrowden – its neighbour over in Rutland – can be seen these curious brick towers.

Situated in area rich in limestone, these were calcine kilns for burning stone down to powdered quicklime. Except they didn't. Erected in the First World War, there were meant to be four, complete with a tramway and tipping dock on the railway. Only two were built (the bases for the others can be seen), 23.4 metres (77 feet) high and 10 metres (33 feet) in diameter, but they never felt the roar of the furnaces sucking air in through the semicircular openings. They're not exactly a beautiful addition to the very rural landscape round here, but as time has mellowed them they sit very comfortably amongst the grazing sheep. I would miss them dearly if they went.

Bliss Tweed Mill, Chipping Norton, Oxfordshire

Coming into Chipping Norton on the Stow-on-the-Wold road, this 1872 mill is unmissable, rising above the hedge at the foot of a steeply sloping pasture where cows contentedly graze. The building is certainly impressive, a classic expression of contemporary wealth and power. But just look at that chimney. Is this Willie Wonka's chocolate factory? It must be, with that sink plunger addition to the skyline, a stone chimneystack on an ecclesiastical lead dome pointing up into the Oxfordshire clouds. The architect was George Woodhouse, probably more at ease on his home patch of Lancashire, where he made sure that the mills and factories of his clients dominated the terraced homes of their clog-wearing workers.

above
**Tweed in the Cotswolds
at Chipping Norton**

opposite
**Northamptonshire
curiosities at Wakerley**

Nutley Windmill, East Sussex

Our first windmills would have looked something like this, and also been post mills. Often seen in medieval manuscripts with peasants staggering up to them with heavy sacks on their backs, the earliest illustration of one is to be found in the *Windmill Psalter* (*c* 1270).

Nutley is a village on the edge of the Ashdown Forest, 'Winnie the Pooh Country' for those who love these things. My family and I first discovered this classic post mill on a cold and windy Easter Monday, following signs that pointed down a path through gorse bushes from the Forest. To everyone's amazement we could see the sails turning behind the trees, a fairy-tale scene reminiscent of Neil Jordan's film *The Company of Wolves*. We were invited in and I shall never forget the looks of both amazement and apprehension on the children's faces as the entire structure shook and rattled in the wind.

The very nature of these post mills means that they are comparatively easy to move, and there exist many instances of the same mill appearing in different locations: the mills at Thorpeness in Suffolk and Madingley in Cambridgeshire come to mind. Nutley Mill was moved very likely from Kilndown in Kent not long before 1840 when miller Henry Selford was grinding corn for smallholders here; its structure is believed to be around 300 years old.

Saxtead Green Post Mill, Suffolk

Perched on its roundhouse, the 1796 Saxtead Green Post Mill is a reminder of the times when sails would have turned against the sky, milling the corn from surrounding fields. The main structure here is called a 'buck' and it turns in the direction of the wind on a single timber post by the use of the vertically oriented fantail, one of the first pieces of automatic machinery. Here at Saxtead Green the blue-finned fantail revolves around with the mill, attached to the exterior ladder that runs on a track circuiting the roundhouse. It has been known to move with an unexpected change of wind direction, only to end up crashing into an unfortunately parked car. The English Heritage lady and I had a good time wondering what was put on the insurance claim – 'hit by moving windmill' sounds so unlikely.

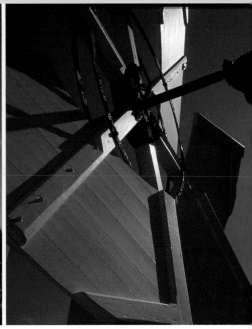

This is an archetypal tower mill in a near-perfect setting, seven miles east of Dersingham in Norfolk. Standing proudly over the pantiled roofs of its ancillary buildings, and with the smell of freshly baked bread wafting from the bakery, all it needs is a goose girl in a pale blue smock shooing her charges past in the meadow. This 1846 mill worked until the 1920s but was derelict 50 years later. It has been beautifully restored to full working order by John Lawn, complete with a coat of black resin known as Bellecoat Stipple and a new cap topped-out with its finial. I found it very rewarding on the hot afternoon of my visit to step out on to the wooden balcony and see the big sweeps framing the countryside steeped in heat for miles around, and then finally to reach the top and see the fantail motionless against the blue sky.

Shipley Windmill, West Sussex

Smock mills are so-called because of their resemblance to the tent-like garments once worn by farm labourers. The 1879 Shipley Windmill is the largest, albeit youngest, such mill in Sussex, variously called King's Mill, Vincent's Mill and, the one I like best, Mrs Shipley. It is also named Belloc's Mill after French writer Hilaire Belloc who lived nearby from 1906. In 1958 restoration was completed by the county council in his memory, noted on a plaque attached to the mill: 'Let this be a memorial to Hilaire Belloc who garnered a harvest of wisdom and sympathy for young and old.' I also like the trim petticoat around the sail cap, neatly scalloped like a railway station valance, and the fact that the first millwright here was called Mr Grist.

opposite left
Bircham Windmill

opposite right
Fantail of restored mill

right
Shipley smock windmill, east of Billingshurst in West Sussex

Post Office Tower, London

This steel and glass cylinder is the landmark that marks the transition from General Post Office to British Telecom, from green telephone vans and tarred poles to microwave aerials and worldwide communications. Replacing a 1940s steel lattice tower on the roof of the nearby Museum telephone exchange, it was designed by Eric Bedford and GR Yeats from the Ministry of Public Buildings and Works, built by Peter Lind & Company and opened by Prime Minister Harold Wilson on 8 October 1965. The 'white heat' of 1960s technology, a London icon to go with mini cars and mini skirts.

The main tower is 177 metres (581 feet) tall, with additional aerials bringing the overall height to 189 metres (620 feet). It is perhaps best remembered today for the posh revolving Top of the Tower restaurant – one revolution every 22 minutes – and the IRA attack in October 1971 when a bomb went off in the men's toilets. Thankfully there were no injuries: the only person in the tower was a security guard who was lifted out of the seat of his chair. Closed to the public since 1981, it nevertheless often stands in as an alternative to the Big Ben clock tower as an establishing London landmark – in anything from the Ford Anglia flight in *Harry Potter and the Chamber of Secrets* to the front cover image for Ian McEwan's novel *Saturday*. And up until the mid-1990s its very existence was an official secret, not marked on any maps. But it does exist, at 60 Cleveland Street.

Express Lift Tower, Northampton

Northampton is so proud of this tower it has thus far resisted all attempts to pull it down. As far as I'm aware even the homeowners whose houses have been built perilously near to its base have affection for it. Dubbed 'the Northampton Lighthouse' by Terry Wogan, it first rose above the town in 1980 in order to test lifts and all the bits and pieces that go with them, and to train staff in their use and maintenance. Within the 127.4-metre- (418-foot-) tall tower, designed by architect Maurice Walton, are three separate shafts, and a lift could be dropped down within one at the terrifying speed of 7 metres (23 feet) a second, which if you're in it must mean all your clothing is left at the top. Queen Elizabeth II opened it in 1982; it is not recorded whether or not Her Majesty tried it out at full speed. The Express Lift Company was absorbed into Otis in 1997 and the tower closed.

right
A monstrous garden ornament for a new estate of houses

opposite
The BT Tower from a Fitzrovia side street

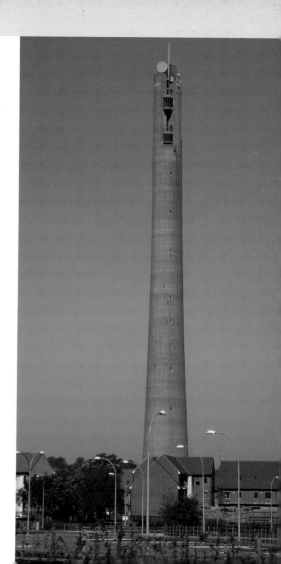

Like cooling towers, sugar beet silos and flour mills are unsung heroes of the landscape. Many may think that 'blots' is a more apt description, but there can be no doubt that they have a bold and uncompromising presence. The sugar beet silos near Newark in Nottinghamshire dominate the flatlands by the River Trent, providing a vast storage capacity for sugar processed from the root crop grown in the area. Operations began here in 1921, and although the harvesting starts in mid-September, the country's crop beet continues to grow at 10,000 tons of sugar a day. That's an awful lot of teaspoonfuls, but to stand inside an empty silo is to experience a curious oppressive silence and a sense that at any moment you might be completely submerged in sugar.

Silos are a prime example of form following function, much as flour mills impress as simple elegant containers, with little relief in the way of windows or exterior decoration. The kind of structure we'd expect to be more at home out on a Kansas prairie, Corby Flour Mill is the Northamptonshire location for ADM, the biggest UK independent millers. In the same county I always look out for Heygates Flour Mills at Bugbrooke at the side of the M1 motorway near junction 16, where an astonishing 200,000 tons of wheat are milled every year, producing 150,000 tons of flour. The buildings here date from the late 19th century to the early 21st.

opposite top
British Sugar's silos at Newark, Nottinghamshire

opposite bottom
Corby Flour Mills, Northamptonshire

above
Heygates Flour Mills at Bugbrooke, Northamptonshire

Millennium Mills and Grain Silo 'D', North Woolwich, London

These gaunt mills are one of the last reminders of that vast area of East London that was docklands. Real, working docks, as one saw in the background of films like *The Long Good Friday*, before the penthouses, exhibition centres and Gotham City skyscrapers rose up above the oily waters. Spillers' Millennium Mills are a true survivor, the unbowed boxer avoiding the knock-out punch on the Royal Victoria Dock. Their origins were in the new mill built for Vernon & Sons in 1933, the north elevation being added in 1954. What must it have been like down here on a working day – the shriek of steam whistles, the cries of dockers high up on openings and cranes, the thunder of Fodens and Albions loaded with white cotton flour sacks manoeuvring out on to arterial roads.

Immediately to the south is a reinforced concrete grain silo. Here bulk grain was lifted from ships and barges, deposited inside and then weighed before being redistributed into other barges. This 1920 tower replaced corrugated iron silos that received extensive damage in the Silvertown explosion of 1917.

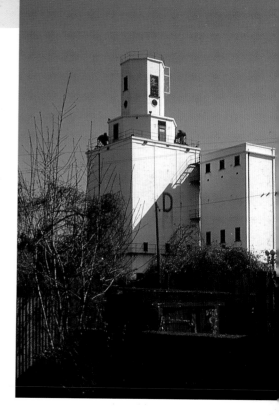

opposite top
The south elevation of the Millennium Mills

opposite bottom
The north elevation on the Royal Victoria Dock

right
Grain Silo 'D' watching over the new housing estates and roads of North Woolwich

above
Sir Owen Williams's 1932 Boots Factory

right
Details of the classic 1932 glass and concrete building, both functional and pleasing to the eye

The Beeston headquarters of Boots the Chemists is more small town than a disparate collection of factories and offices. Tree-lined roads take traffic round a succession of roundabouts and junctions until the *pièce de résistance* is reached on the far side, the ground-breaking buildings by Sir Owen Williams. The first is something we will be very familiar with now, the glass-walled structure that would today be an office block. But this is 1932, and the building housed Boots girls busy in a great top-lit packing hall –'like a huge department store', as Nikolaus Pevsner says in his *Buildings of England: Nottinghamshire*. This is one of the first adventures in concrete and glass, and is still immensely pleasing.

Next door is a 1938 building that is more Art Deco French Riviera hotel than factory, and although not as lauded by the architectural *cognoscenti* as the earlier factory it is nevertheless a stunning workplace. Both buildings reflect what must be two of Boots' ideals: that of healthy, clean living not only for their customers, but just as importantly for their workforce.

right
Sir Owen Williams's 1938 Boots Factory

above
**The Lego-inspired
Container City**

above right
**Staircase detail at
Container City**

opposite
**Lightship at Trinity Buoy
Wharf**

On the opposite bank of the Thames to the Dome (as we're now not supposed to call it) is an airy wharf with a lightship and a lighthouse built for Michael Faraday to test electric lighting. A favoured location for TV programme *The Bill*, the wharf is also home to Container City, low-cost workplaces made from corrugated steel shipping containers. Developers Urban Space Management, architects Nicholas Lacey & Partners and engineers Buro Happold, who started the project in 2000, extended the maritime feel by putting in windows reminiscent of portholes.

At five storeys high, the resultant structure remains rigid, even with steel only 2 millimetres (just over 1/16 inch) thick and each container weighing in at 4 tons. The masterstroke is painting them all in bright colours, so perfectly at home here amongst the warning-coloured nauticalia. I wonder, do the new occupants ponder over where their new workspaces have been – once full, perhaps, of cameras from China or china from Cambodia?

Newton Water Tower, Cambridgeshire

This water tower sits out in the bleak landscape at Newton, where Cambridgeshire narrows to a point up near The Wash. It is a simple unadorned landmark structure that has enormous appeal for its functional simplicity, coupled with the fact that thought was given to its placement here by planting a stand of silver birch and willow around it. Water towers are necessary where natural gradients are insufficient to maintain a good head of water, and, like all things, the acceptability of their presence in isolated countryside comes down to design. There are stunning examples – the landmark towers of Ravensden in Bedfordshire (1953) and the 1920s Wellsian science-fiction Mappleton out on the Plain of Holderness in Yorkshire. You probably wouldn't want one looking over your back garden, but necessity can still be the mother of inventive design. I suppose it comes down to taste, like good old-fashioned tap water versus overpriced 'eau' run-off from your local volcano.

far right
The Newton Water Tower, Cambridgeshire

right
The Ravensden Water Tower on a bend in the road in Bedfordshire

Appleton Water Tower, West Newton, Norfolk

I suppose it's inevitable that a water tower on a royal estate is going to show itself off. This tower doesn't hide its function – a cast-iron water tank supported on a local carstone octagon complete with a viewing tower – and was erected here in response to the eldest son of the Prince of Wales (the future Edward VII) being struck down with typhoid fever, brought about by a dodgy water supply at Sandringham. Designed by Robert Rawlinson, erection of the tower started in July 1877 after the foundation stone was laid by the Princess of Wales. It was immediately the centre of a right royal row when a tenant farmer complained about the damage caused by construction traffic.

The octagon contained the caretaker's living accommodation, and his homely fires kept the water from freezing. These days the water tower makes a very eccentric addition to the catalogue of properties looked after by the inestimable Landmark Trust, who restore such remarkable buildings as holiday lets, so its eccentricities can now be enjoyed by all.

right top
**The Appleton Water Tower
for the Sandringham Estate**

right
**The Mappleton Water
Tower, built for Hornsea
Council in the 1920s in the
East Riding of Yorkshire**

BRITANNIA

Goole has more than its fair share of intriguing structures. This uncompromising east-coast port lies some distance inland, far up the Humber Estuary and on one of the last river bends of the Yorkshire Ouse. Towering over the red brick terraces and port paraphernalia are these two water towers. But what an odd couple they are, known locally as the Salt and Pepper Pots. The Victorian red brick tower, opened in July 1883, supports an iron sphere that looks like a cannonball stuffed into the breech, or an immense sinister ball cock that might suddenly decide to roll off down into the terraced streets. It proved inadequate for the expanding Goole population, so the simply gargantuan ferroconcrete tower was built next to it in 1926. At the time this was, unsurprisingly, the largest ever built. But it's the juxtaposition of the two towers (one could never describe these two as 'twins') that amazes. It's as if Goole had said: 'This is where we put water towers. Always have, always will.'

left
Goole's 'Salt & Pepper Pots' towering over the port

far right
Green monster of Goole Docks, once able to move about the quays at will, now impotently pinned-down

right
Goole cranes, silos and a Danish ship from Faaborg

Coal Hoist, Goole, East Riding of Yorkshire

This is one of those erections you simply can't ignore, so alien to one's normal architectural sensibilities, but so much of an unconscious statement about what makes a hard working place like Goole tick. It is a coal hoist, built some time between 1880 and 1910, and it once bodily lifted 'Tom Pudding' compartment boats into the air so that South Yorkshire coal could be deposited into freighters. It was one of five, but this pale green giant was able to be floated to wherever it was wanted. Immobilised now and screwed down to the dock, it is thankfully Grade II listed and a roost for at least 200 pigeons. The little iron lighthouse was the control room.

Corrugated Iron Structures

Ubiquitous, neglected and much maligned, corrugated iron gets a bad press, probably because of its make-do-and-mend properties and perceived second-rate-ness as a building material. But looked at in another way it actually adds as much to the English vernacular scene as stone, thatch, brick and tile. In 1828 Henry Robinson Palmer was the first to realise that corrugating iron increased its tensile strength, and that galvanising the metal protected it from oxidising. So any corrugated iron that shows signs of rust really has been around for a long time.

Its use as a prefabricated material meant that buildings could be put up cheaply and quickly – not just radial-roofed Dutch barns, but everything from village halls to complete houses, finished off in any colour on the paint chart. Instant townships arrived at far-flung outposts of the British Empire on cargo ships; churches and chapels (tin tabernacles) were sent out in flat packs that could be summoned by mail order from Harrods, complete with ticked-off items on the accessory list such as wooden porches and bellcotes. A versatile material that means that we can appreciate some truly charming and idiosyncratic buildings wherever we live.

left top
Garden shed, Slawston, Leicestershire

right top
Church Hall, Blandford Forum, Dorset

left
Green's Lodge, near Whissendine, Rutland

above
Field barn near Halstead, Leicestershire

right
Goadby, Leicestershire

far right centre
Dutch barn, Saxby, Leicestershire

far right bottom
Derelict barn next to cricket pitch in Hallaton, Leicestershire

De VILLE & LEAR
ENGINEERS
ROSTON
NR. ASHBOURNE

bridges

Brand identity for the
Industrial Revolution:
the 1779 Iron Bridge in
Shropshire, cast to the
designs of architect
Thomas Farnolls
Pritchard by local
ironmaster Abraham
Darby. The world's first
iron bridge, spanning a
steeply wooded gorge on
the River Severn

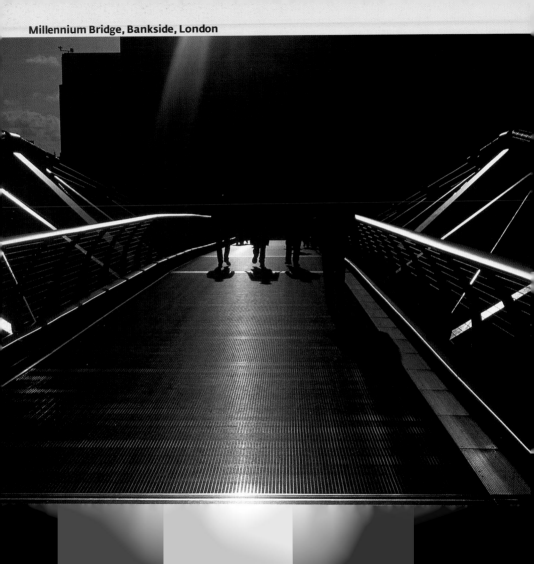
Millennium Bridge, Bankside, London

Designed by Arup, Foster & Partners and Sir Anthony Caro, this Millennium Bridge is probably the first one to come to mind. But, because of a quirk of physics, it was also dubbed the Wobbly Bridge on its inauspicious opening on 10 June 2000. This was the result of 'Synchronous Lateral Excitation' which is what happens when the natural sway of people walking across the bridge sets up small sideways oscillations that become amplified to cause the wobble effect. Great news for the press, not so good for the engineers, but now it's all been sorted out and the bridge is perfectly stable. This was the first bridge across the Thames in London since the opening of Tower Bridge in 1894, and connects Tate Modern (originally the Bankside Power Station) with St Paul's Cathedral.

opposite
View towards Tate Modern

right top
St.Paul's and the Millennium Bridge

right centre
Detail of suspension struts

right bottom
View from Bankside

Menai Bridge, Isle of Anglesey

Here at the shortest crossing point of the Menai Straits between Anglesey and Gwynedd is Thomas Telford's great suspension bridge. The original giant links were forged in Shropshire, and in April 1825 they were transported from near Shrewsbury on the newly opened Shropshire Union Canal to Chester, thence around the coast to the Straits. A pipe band and quarts of ale accompanied their positioning on the pylons constructed from stone brought from the nearby Penmon quarries. A stormy night in the following January saw it officially opened, another stupendous achievement on Telford's London to Holyhead road, the last public turnpike to be built. As the first horses' hooves clattered over the original wooden decking pulling the Irish Mail coach, the journey time between the road's English and Welsh termini had been reduced from 36 hours to 27 – a journey that today takes a little over five hours.

Marlow Suspension Bridge, Buckinghamshire

Marlow's elegant suspension bridge was started in 1829 by John Millington, but on his departure to America was finished by William Tierney Clark in 1832 – the same year that the predecessor of the bridge's Thames-side companion, the parish church, was demolished (it was replaced three years later to designs by CF Inwood). One does wonder if the bridge's arched pylons were influenced by Sir John Soane's late-18th-century gateway to Tyringham Hall in the same county. Clark first worked at the Coalbrookdale Ironworks in Shropshire where the world's first iron bridge was cast, and also designed the first Hammersmith Bridge. The acclaim for his Marlow bridge was such that he was commissioned to build the suspension bridge across the Danube in Budapest, which closely resembles it.

But forget Hungarian lookalikes, this is a classic River Thames destination. At its heart an 18th-century market town with many attractions, down on the waterside it's Victorian. The bridge will be remembered fondly as the place in *Three Men in a Boat* where Jerome K Jerome's intrepid scullers first attempted to escape the all-pervading smell of paraffin oil that had 'oozed' from their stove.

opposite
The Menai Suspension Bridge from the Gwynedd shore

right
Marlow Suspension Bridge and All Saints' Church

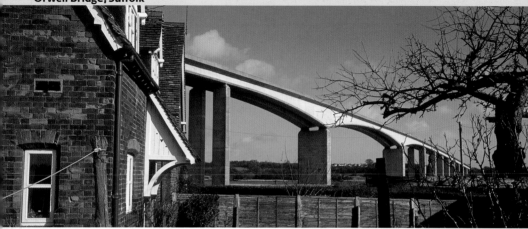

Traffic anxious to get to the Suffolk coast will soar over the River Orwell on this spectacular bridge, but unless you're high up in the cab of a lorry you won't see much of the surrounding landscape. Parapets are made high so that car drivers don't get distracted, but it's certainly worth taking a detour down to the Shotley peninsula to see the graceful arches from ground level. Modern bridges don't normally inspire affection, but this one has found a deserved place in the hearts of East Anglians, even in the little red brick cottage that snuggles up to it at Wherstead. The engineers were Sir William Halcrow & Partners, and it was opened much to the relief of the streets of Ipswich in 1982.

top and above
The Orwell Bridge from Wherstead

Ouse Valley Viaduct, Balcombe, West Sussex

From an electric train speeding down to Brighton from London, all that one will see of this stunning structure are the two groups of four Italianate pavilions at each end. They were designed by David Mocatta in 1841 as the finishing touches to JU Rastrick's 29-metre- (96-foot-) high viaduct, striding over the wooded valley of the gentle River Ouse on 37 red brick arches. This is often considered to be the finest viaduct in southern England, and is best seen in all its glory from a little back road leading north of Haywards Heath to the village of Balcombe. For an alternative view, take a look at John Piper's endpaper for the Shell Guide to East Sussex (the boundary between East and West appears prone to movement). Piper pointed his camera through the receding perspective of the radial-cornered openings in the brick piers, a photograph that could be either way up.

right top
The spectacular Ouse Valley Viaduct on the London to Brighton line

right
One of David Mocatta's pavilions on the Ouse Valley Viaduct, and a detail of the succession of arches

Clifton Suspension Bridge, Bristol

Whichever way you approach it, the Clifton Suspension Bridge induces gasps of astonishment, if not awe. Probably the best view is from the River Avon, looking seawards from Bristol, or on the road in from Avonmouth. It was the brainchild of Isambard Kingdom Brunel, the most celebrated engineer of the Victorian age, but all he saw in his lifetime were two pylons and a bucket on a cable that Bristol folk would pay five shillings to ride in, 76.2 metres (250 feet) above the Avon Gorge. Finished in 1864, it is full of drama, albeit differing from Brunel's original design and without the stone sphinxes that he had wanted to lie on the towers.

The suspension chains, bought for the bargain price of £5,000 from the old Hungerford Bridge in London, are anchored in the rock of the gorge. If you decide to jump off (there's a Samaritans phone number at the entrances) your chances of survival are very slim. However, a Victorian would-be suicide, who descended whilst clasping her child to her bosom, was saved by her crinoline opening like a parachute.

Whilst not exactly as Brunel first conceived it, this Bristol landmark bridge was completed with unanimous fervour by his friends, colleagues and rivals as a fitting memorial to his genius.

Queen Elizabeth II Bridge, Dartford, Kent

The Queen Elizabeth II Bridge was opened on 30 October 1991, much to the relief of traffic previously funnelled into the two road tunnels. Everyone thinks that the M25 is a complete circuit, but in fact there's a break here and the road becomes the A282 for the crossings. Most views for motorists will be on their southbound journeys – a few minutes' aerial view of the Thames, a power station and container ships straining at their mooring jetties.

But walk along the riverside path from Greenhithe and all the astounding statistics come to neck-craning life. 145,000 cubic metres (over 5 million cubic feet) of concrete, 190,000 tons of structural steel, 750,000 high-strength bolts and 112 cables weighing 15 tons each. The pylons soar upwards for 137 metres (449 feet) above the river; the paint order was for 221,850 litres (48,800 gallons). £86 million to build it, £1 to cross it in your car. Good value, I feel.

opposite
The Clifton Suspension Bridge from the Downs

right
The Queen Elizabeth II Bridge from the Greenhithe shore in Kent

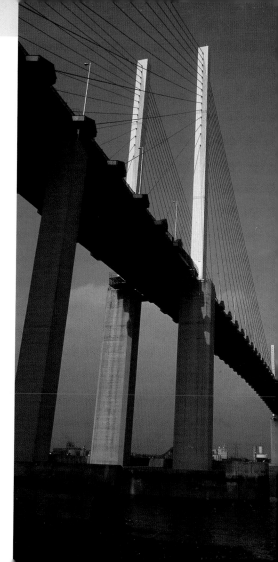

High Level Bridge, Newcastle Upon Tyne

Arriving at the River Tyne between Newcastle and Gateshead is like visiting a Festival of Bridges. Lined up in such close proximity, they are a stunning history of Tyne Crossings, the first being the High Level Bridge that carries both rail (on top) and road (below) in and out of the heart of Newcastle city centre. Designed for the York, Newcastle & Berwick Railway by Robert Stephenson and TE Harrison, and completed in 1849, the bridge transformed the economy of the locality by bringing Gateshead within easy communication. It is formed by six cast-iron arches between masonry piers that support the railway tracks with hollow columns, whilst the approach viaducts are formed more traditionally with round-headed arches carrying the road, and further cast-iron columns in arcades supporting the trackbed. It all works magnificently, and was opened when Queen Victoria and Prince Albert's royal train stopped on the bridge during a return journey from Balmoral.

left
**Bridgefest in
Newcastle, framed by
the road and rail High
Level Bridge**

above
The Tyne Bridge from the parapet of the adjacent Swing Bridge

opposite
View from the Gateshead shore

If there was ever such an emphatic trademark for Newcastle, this is surely it. For years before I saw the Tyne Bridge I gazed at its silhouette on the blue star of numerous Newcastle Brown Ale bottle labels, the so-familiar steel arch strung out between two towers of Cornish stone. The bottle now gives pride of place to the new Millennium Bridge. Connections are inevitably made between the Tyne Bridge and the somewhat larger Australian version at Sydney Harbour, and indeed the latter was designed by the Newcastle bridge's contractors Dorman Long. The design credit here on Tyneside belongs to Mott, Hay & Anderson, and construction over the Tyne started in 1925. King George V opened the finished bridge in October 1928, and the original green paint finish has now been restored.

The road deck is 25.6 metres (84 feet) above water, the span 161.8 metres (531 feet), and the cost was £1,200,000. There was an original intention to use the towers as warehouses, but the floors never got put in. They did, however, act as lift shafts. Many buildings were demolished to make way for the bridge, including a pickle factory, a bank, and notably four public houses: the Goat Inn, the Earl of Durham, the Ridley Arms and the Steamboat Inn. One wonders if the disenfranchised drinkers toasted the bridge's opening with bottles of Newcastle Brown, introduced just the year before.

This is the world's first tilting bridge, a pair of steel arches that open and close like a winking eye in order to let shipping pass through on the River Tyne between Gateshead and Newcastle. One arch is the deck, the other supports it with suspension wires. Designed by Wilkinson Eyre Architects and Gifford & Partners, and constructed by Watson Steel of Bolton, it gave its first wink in June 2001. Each tilt takes just four minutes, and it is apparently so energy efficient that each opening costs only £3.60. As can be seen, or not, I got there too late to see it doing its trick, but even if a ship isn't wanting to go through there are often single performances just to amuse passers-by, presumably after they've cleared the decking. And if they ever take it down there's enough steel in here to make 64 double-decker buses or 16 Chieftain tanks.

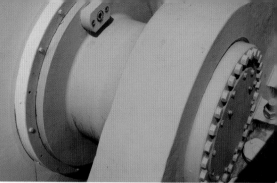

above
The Gateshead Millennium Bridge from The Sage music centre

left
The suspension arch

top
One of the business ends of the tilt mechanism

opposite
View downriver from the Newcastle Swing Bridge, with the Baltic art gallery on the right

opposite and above
The York Millennium Bridge from opposing banks of the Ouse

left
Attention to detail: suspension wire tensioner and parapet railings

Walk southwards from Rowntree Park on the banks of the River Ouse, and this seductive curve greets the eye, the first permanent bridge at the site. In 1996 York schoolchildren entered a competition to consider what sort of crossing could be here, and the results formed the inspiration for this Millennium Bridge. The designers and consultant engineers were Whitby Bird & Partners, and the bridge was opened by the Duke of York in May 2001. Designed primarily as a pedestrian and cycle link, the gravity-defying curves also clearly define a focal point and meeting place for local residents, as evidenced by wooden seating running down its entire length. What a delightful way to enjoy the view.

Great Central Railway Viaduct, Leicester

The Great Central Railway (GCR) was the last main railway line to be built, from Annesley in Nottinghamshire to Quainton Road in Buckinghamshire. Opened in 1899, it connected the northern railways of chairman Sir Edward Watkin with a joint line developed with the Metropolitan Railway into London. Watkin's dream was for a fast route across the Pennines, the Midlands and the capital to a Channel tunnel and on to Paris. The GCR ran out of steam in Marylebone, a tiny station by comparison with other London termini, and in less than 70 years the fast 'London Extension' across Midland acres had gone.

The GCR crossed high above the historical heart of Leicester on a succession of viaducts, many of which still remain. The most impressive straddles the Old River Soar, a magnificent bowstring lattice girder leviathan, and at the time of writing is under threat of extinction by Leicester City Council because its neighbour, De Montfort University, needs to extend its sports facilities. I travelled on this line in the 1960s, and never in my wildest imaginings did I think that in the future one of its most outstanding landmarks could disappear so that there was more room to play netball and swim. What's wrong with the canal?

Cross Keys Bridge, Lincolnshire

Six miles from its outfall into The Wash, the River Nene approaches Sutton Bridge. Here is one of my favourite bridges, the third 19th-century manifestation constructed at the location to take both a main road (now the busy A17 Sleaford to Boston) and a railway across the river, navigable up to Wisbech. The uninterrupted passage of ships necessitates a swing bridge, which still allows the odd Dutch freighter further upstream.

The hydraulically powered swing bridge was built by A Handyside & Co of Derby in 1894–7, at a cost of £80,000. The railway closed in 1965, freeing up for use what is now the westbound carriageway, and I hear that plans are now afoot to convert the operating cabin into a talking-piece home. The hydraulics are still in a neighbouring tower. Another eccentricity can be seen on the road that runs just south of the bridge next to the river, a sign on the grass verge that intriguingly says 'Please Dip Headlights When Ships Are Approaching'.

opposite
The Great Central Railway viaduct over the old River Soar, Leicester

right
The Cross Keys Bridge taking the A17 over the River Nene

Lancaster, Millennium Bridge, Lancashire

The twin masts of the cable stays on Lancaster's Millennium Bridge are immediately evocative of the tall masts of ships that would once have worked their way up the River Lune to the docks. That's what I love about this bridge, a state-of-the-art design that's perfectly at home in this heritage-centred environment. It's only for pedestrians and cyclists (one of whom ran me over) but engineers Whitby Bird have produced something remarkable for the city that only acts to reinforce the nature of Lancaster's historic quayside. The Y shape has gangways anchored to the shore that minimise sway. In 2005 the design and construction was awarded a Sustrans National Cycle Network Award for Excellence.

Merchants Bridge, Castlefield, Manchester

There are no less than eight bridges in this area, cataloguing over 200 years of Manchester's industrial heritage. Railways and canals, boats and trains, pedestrians and cyclists, all converge at the Bridgewater Canal's Castlefield Basin. And in complete contrast to the iron and brick heavyweight neighbours is Whitby Bird's Merchants Bridge, the winner of a hotly contested competition to provide a new crossing at this point. Or, as night-life-indulging Mancunians will tell you, a quicker way to get from the Quay Bar to the Barça Café Bar in Catalan Square.

But the bridge has become more than an expression of fast-developing technologies creating a confident unique form. Merchants Bridge has also become a focus and symbol for the regeneration of an area once teeming with the lifeblood of Manchester's industry. Whitby Bird have been showered with awards since its completion in 1995, including a Civic Trust Award and, although not very evident from these pictures, a National Lighting Design Award.

opposite
Whitby Bird's Millennium Bridge for Lancaster's cyclists and walkers

right
Manchester's Merchants Bridge at the Castlefield Basin on the Bridgewater Canal

Welland Valley Viaduct, Harringworth, Northamptonshire

This viaduct is simply colossal, always in the eye for miles around, and at 1,165 metres (1,275 yards) is the longest in Britain outside of London. The area is naturally boggy, and they say a million sheepskins were laid down before construction could begin. There are 82 arches, costing a thousand pounds each in 1879, and it was built in blue engineering bricks, now patched in red.

There are differing local opinions as to what it's called. Two villages lie at each end, Harringworth in Northamptonshire and Seaton over in Rutland. The Welland is the counties' border, and rumour has it that a tug-of-war once took place over the river. Whichever village won, it claimed the right for the viaduct to take its name. So you will hear Harringworth Viaduct and Seaton Viaduct as much as

you will Welland Valley. Harringworth steals a march by installing altar kneelers in the church of St John Baptist embroidered with most of the viaduct and a diverted blue and yellow InterCity train going over it.

Kingsferry Bridge, Isle of Sheppey, Kent

These giant croquet hoops support both a rail and road bridge that lifts vertically up over The Swale to allow water traffic in and out of Ridham Dock. There is now a new road bridge, but a local road still runs next to the railway, both serving traffic traversing between the Kent mainland and the Isle of Sheppey. The engineer hides in one of the hoops, and if you're on a yacht and display a coloured bucket on your mast, the bridge will be lifted for you. Or so they say. Local feeling ran high when there was only the one carriageway for the heavy traffic arriving and departing from the island and Sheerness docks, when a wait of 25 minutes was not uncommon. The Kingsferry Bridge was built in 1960 and designed by Mott, Hay & Anderson.

above
The Kingsferry Bridge taking both the railway and the A249 across The Swale

opposite
The Royal Albert crossing the Tamar between Plymouth and Saltash

Royal Albert Bridge, Saltash, Cornwall

The cigar-smoking, top-hatted Brunel brought his railway across the River Tamar, and joined Devon with Cornwall with what in 1859 must have looked like a structure sent from a distant future. The brief was for a 335.2-metre (1,100-foot) crossing that still allowed 30.4 metres (100 feet) of headroom for sailing ships, and the solution is the only railway-carrying semi-suspension bridge in the world. The trackbed is suspended from two giant wrought-iron tubes, floated down the river on specially constructed pontoons. With much semaphore flag waving the hushed crowds on the opposing banks watched as they were guided into position and lifted up between the stone piers. At the brass band-playing inauguration, the bridge, named after the Prince Consort, saw the seriously ill engineer laid on a bed in an open truck and gently carried over so that he could look up and see his masterpiece. His name is immortalised high up on the portals at either end.

Made famous by appearances in both the film *Billy Elliot* and the TV series *AufWeidersehen, Pet*, the Middlesbrough Transporter Bridge is so defining of the city that it takes pride of place on the Council badge. In 1911 a bridge was required here that gave access to Port Clarence and yet still gave headway for tall-masted ships. The problem was solved by engineers Sir William Arrol & Co by suspending a gondola from a 48.7-metre-(160-foot-) high gantry by what are known as trolley wires, in order that this strange craft could ply (as it still does) across the River Tees with foot passengers and up to nine cars. The hair-raising ascent is like going up into the clouds through a gargantuan Meccano model, the view back down to the water through open-mesh steel flooring very unnerving. Particularly when you see the gondola silently moving below with perhaps just a lone seagull gliding through. But it is all very assuringly safe, and certainly the bridge's endurance record is impressive, having survived air raids in two world wars.

right
The gondola approaches the south shore of the River Tees

opposite
Aerial view from the gantry walkway

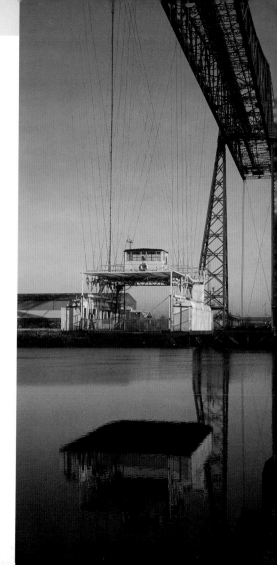

Forth Bridge, Edinburgh

After the Tay Bridge disaster of 1879, when an inadequate structure collapsed and pitched a train and 79 passengers into the estuary, the construction of the 1890 Forth Bridge needed to be a belt-and-braces job. And what belts and braces they are. Three double cantilevers, with 518-metre- (1,700-foot-) long suspended spans between them, are able to withstand extraordinary wind pressures and are held together by 6,500,000 rivets. I was very fortunate to be taken up to the top when the massive restoration programme was underway, when all the layers of the myth-making repainting were being stripped off and oil rig marine paint in the original colour applied.

The men responsible were Sir John Fowler and Sir Benjamin Baker, the latter engaged in most of the design. Is there a more immediately recognisable railway bridge? A massive red insect stretching over the steel-blue waters of the Firth of Forth; look out for it not only from the Forth Road Bridge, but also from your aeroplane as it circles round to Edinburgh airport.

opposite
The Forth Bridge from the Firth of Forth

right
Views from the top during restoration

Findhorn Viaduct, Tomatin, Highland

Between Perth and Inverness the railway passes through some of the most spectacular scenery in Britain, including the summits at Slochd (400 metres / 1,315 feet) and Druimuachdar (452 metres / 1,484 feet), making this the highest main line in Britain. In 1897 Murdoch Paterson built this viaduct over the River Findhorn for the Highland Railway, nine 36.5-metre- (120-foot-) span latticed steel girders carried on a magnificent succession of tapered masonry piers.

The Highland Railway revolutionised the transport of freight in this inhospitable region, and this imposing viaduct would once have thundered to the vibrations of big Drummond 4-4-0 locomotives

pulling trucks of fish from remote northern coasts, whisky from the new distilleries built near the line and cattle from wherever the beasts could be loaded. The railway worked hard to develop tourism, particularly for the seasonal traffic of moving shooting parties to their grouse moors.

above left
Snow on the River Findhorn

above right
 Viaduct pier in Tomatin

opposite right
The Heyop Valley, Powys

opposite left
Norman details at Knucklas

Knucklas Viaduct, Powys

Built for the Central Wales Railway in 1864 by Henry Robertson, this 173-metre- (190-yard-) long viaduct resembles something the Normans might have built, had they needed such a structure. It crosses a tributary of the River Teme on 13 arches, and has buttresses that turn themselves into square and round towers, complete with cruciform arrow slits. To repel sieges by rival railway companies, perhaps, they were most likely added at the request of local landowners the Pryce-Greens.

Travelling on the little train southwards through the Welsh Border country from Shrewsbury, you will cross the viaduct after Knucklas station at the start of the Heyop Valley. Coming from the other direction, look out for it after Llangunllo. The location is almost impossibly picturesque, the rough grey stonework in stark contrast with the dark green of the surrounding trees.

Tower Bridge, London

Completed in 1894, this is London's souvenir bridge, so defining of the riverscape that it appears on everything from teapots to leather bookmarks, and as the crockery emblem at a very expensive restaurant that has the name of the bridge in French, *naturellement*. The competition for designs started in 1876, and went on for eight years until the 1884 entry submitted by City Architect Sir Horace Jones and engineer Sir John Wolfe-Barry was selected. Designed to chime with the Tower of London on the north bank, it featured Armstrong, Mitchell & Co steam pumps to lift the bascules (a hydraulic system now operated by oil and electricity), and had lifts in the towers to access the walkway that gave unparalleled views of the Tower.

Christmas 1935 saw the bascules start to open as a No 78 bus was already at the point of no return. The driver gritted his teeth and accelerated across the ever-widening gap. He was given £10 from public funds, and had a medal pinned on his chest in recognition of his aerial display. This circus act was probably watched by the pigeons who favour the undersides of the bascules for their roosts. Whether by some rapid evolution or ergonomic sensibility, their nests remain secure even when their homes are at the dizzying angle of 80 degrees.

opposite
Tower Bridge from the Pool of London

right
Open bascules

Hammersmith Bridge, London

I love the colour scheme of this suspension bridge over the Thames at Hammersmith. What a treat it is, a green and gold giant designed by Sir Joseph Bazalgette (of sewers fame) on a mission to impress with an exuberant display of detail, and constructed between 1883 and 1887. Massive cast-iron towers are finished off with French pavilion tops and fish-scale roofs, and the steel eyebar chains are anchored in abutments decorated with big gold badges. Every device is brought out of the Heraldry Catalogue: castles and portcullises, horses and lions, crowns and seashells. And lots of gilded oak leaves winding around everything.

The bridge owes its present form to the Oxford and Cambridge University Boat Race, of which this is the midway point. In 1870 much alarm was caused when over 11,000 people crowded onto the predecessor to see the race, and the structure was deemed unsafe. Bazalgette's replacement design was painted in these rich colours, and I do wonder if it's just a coincidence that Lyle's Golden Syrup, in its glorious green and gold can, arrived in the grocers' in 1883, the same year that construction started. These original colours were reinstated after renovations following an IRA bomb attack in 2000.

right top
**The north bank
pylons**

right
**View from the north
shore**

Albert Bridge, Chelsea, London

'Confection' is a much over-used word when writing about fancy architecture, but here at the Albert Bridge between Chelsea and Battersea is surely the right place to use it, yet again. Ian Nairn, in his superbly individual *Nairn's London*, didn't get carried away, calling it 'absurdly over-spiky and over-strutted', which is exactly why we like it. But it does look as though it's been put together in a cake decorating shop, with those seaside blue and pistachio-coloured pylons together with pink icing and cream sponge parapets and stairways.

This rigid suspension bridge, lit up by what look like ordinary household bulbs, was designed by Rowland Mason Ordish and commenced construction in 1870. In post-war London the LCC thought they'd pull it down, but they backed off when confronted by Sir John Betjeman and the population of Chelsea. It will of course be well known for the signs at each end advising troops to break step when marching over it (something to do with vibrations caused by heavy boots and a constant rhythm), where of course 'step' has always been crossed out to be replaced with 'wind'.

right
Details of a staircase and pylon

right top
Ordish's 1871 Albert Bridge on the Thames in West London

Riverside Bridge, Cambridge

Elegant arches are a classic solution in bridge building. Here is the first bridge to span the River Cam in Cambridge since the 1971 Elizabeth Way bridge, connecting the Abbey and Chesterton areas of the city. The multidisciplinary team at Whitby Bird won the contract in 2004, with a deck that divides into two – a footbridge and a cycleway. The footway is constructed from lightweight aluminium planks supported on cantilevered steel arms; the gravel-surfaced cycle path rests on a structural steel box deck. Every material used was chosen for long life and low maintenance, but quite apart from all that it looks simply stunning. And the bridge has the added advantage of being the perfect vantage point to watch rowing events on the Cam.

left, below and opposite
Sculptural elegance on the River Cam, Ramboll Whitby Bird's Riverside Bridge

maritime

Storm clouds gather over
HMS *Belfast* in the Pool of
London. This cruiser was
commissioned into the
Royal Navy on 5 August
1939

Plover Scar Lighthouse, Cockersands, Lancashire

This is a solitary, enchanting shore on the coast of Lancashire between Fleetwood and Heysham. Along the lonely coastal path can be found the battlemented sandstone remains of Cockersands Abbey, once a priory of the Premonstratensians (thankfully also called the White Canons), but the eye here is always drawn to this little sugar-sifter of a lighthouse sitting just out in the waves. It marks the entrance to the River Lune and the docks at Glasson and Lancaster. Built in 1847, this characterful light could be seen for a distance of 11 kilometres (7 miles), and provides the perfect antidote to the grey mass of Heysham nuclear power station on the horizon.

Burnham-on-Sea Lighthouse, Somerset

This multi-legged structure can be found on the sands to the north of Burnham-on-Sea. A 19th-century curate became so possessed with the idea of turning the town into a fashionable spa, he hit on the notion of extracting a toll from ships under passage into the port of Bridgwater in order to raise the necessary funds. This was his 1832 marker. It is not recorded how many ships sailed by with the nautical equivalent of two fingers up in the air, but those that complied only managed to pay for the sinking of trial wells that came to nothing. I think it's marvellously eccentric and heart-warming in its maintenance of such 'nautical style'. I hope it's appreciated as much for its visual appeal as for its convenience as a turning point by the sand yachters racing down the beach from Berrow.

above

The lighthouse on Burnham-on-Sea beach marking the entrance to Bridgwater

opposite

The atmospheric Plover Scar lighthouse at Cockersands

Dungeness Lighthouses, Kent

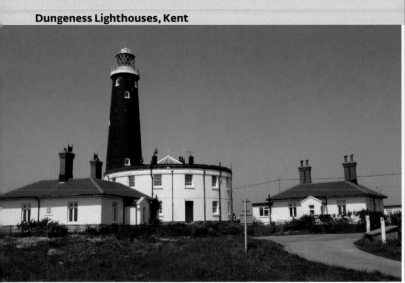

Known since decommissioning in 1960 as The Old Lighthouse (although confusingly once called the 'new' when it superseded Samuel Wyatt's 1792 light, the circular base of which can still be seen here), the black tapering column of 1904 looks out over the 2,400-hectare (6,000-acre) triangle of shingle at Dungeness. A towering landmark in this strange world of uncompromising plants gripping the salt-swept pebbles around tarred huts and single-storey wooden homes, the Old Light is 43.5 metres (143 feet) high, still one of the highest in the United Kingdom. Over three million bricks went into its construction, with slate floors supported on steel beams and

massive rivets. Although HE Bates imagined it as a 'vast white candle in a wide lofty sky' in his short story *The Lighthouse*, his inspiration from this location is unmistakeable.

It has been the Old Lighthouse since the arrival in 1961 of the current light 457 metres (500 yards) to the east. Built because its predecessor became obscured by the nuclear power station, this upturned torch by Ronald Ward & Partners is composed of self-coloured precast rings, and is also externally illuminated as a further aid to shipping. The pattern of squares near the top conceals the fog warning equipment.

North Foreland Lighthouse, Kent

This white wedding cake of a lighthouse appears on a bend of the road between Margate and Broadstairs in Kent. Neatly trimmed hedges lead up to the tower and keepers' cottages, the last manned lighthouse in the country before automation. I was fortunate enough to arrive here as a maintenance crew were changing a light bulb, and so saw the precisely cut reflectors that maximise the eye-scorching power of a grouping of lights, each one appearing to be no bigger than a fat fountain pen. This is the southeast corner of Kent, and indeed England, the lighthouse having guided shipping through the narrow Straits of Dover and into the Thames Estuary since 1691, first with coal, then oil, and now electricity. The last keepers locked the doors on 26 November 1998, bringing to an end a tradition of 300 years' continuous watchful service.

opposite left
The 1904 Dungeness lighthouse

opposite centre
The 1961 Dungenee lighthouse

below left
North Foreland lantern room and lighthouse staircase

below
North Foreland wedding cake lighthouse

Portland Bill Lighthouse, Dorset

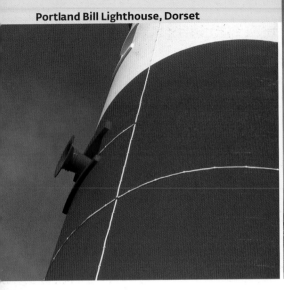

The Isle of Portland is only just attached to the rest of the Dorset coast, by the end of the curious Chesil Beach. A grey, forbidding place even on the brightest of days, this bleak landscape of stone quarries and windswept villages has this classic 1905 red and white striped lighthouse at its southernmost tip. At 41.4 metres (136 feet) high, this is one of the tallest lights in Britain, displaying on its tapered side the protruding mouth of a now sadly silent diaphone foghorn. The lighthouse presides over the notorious race of agitated sea that tumbles between The Bill and the Shambles seabank, towering over the Trinity House seamark obelisk that warns of a dangerous shelf of rock extending out below. Nearby can be seen the towers of two previous lights, the lower now a field centre and bird observatory.

above right
The archetypal lighthouse paint scheme

above left
The diaphone foghorn

South Foreland Lighthouse, Kent

Northeast of Dover at St Margaret's-at-Cliffe is the South Foreland light. It's difficult to find if you're looking for it off the Deal to Dover road, but comes into uninterrupted view if you walk the Saxon Shore Way that passes just below the tower on the cliff edge. Here since 1783, on Christmas Eve 1898 the lighthouse received the world's first ship-to-shore radio transmission. The white pepper-pot lighthouse no longer sends its beams out over the crowded shipping lanes (a fact I find curious, if not slightly disturbing) but it still acts as a daymark for Dover ferries and cross-Channel swimmers. From this point is the shortest distance across the English Channel, 34 kilometres (21 miles).

above
**The South Foreland
lighthouse from the
coastal path**

Is this a Victorian professor's idea of a spacecraft, or a prop from a Wallace and Gromit film? Structures like this, so practical and yet so functional, fire the imagination in as many directions as the beam of light is seen at Blacknore. Built in 1894 by lighthouse board Trinity House to aid shipping as it negotiates the Severn Estuary into Avonmouth, it was converted to electricity in 1941. Another tricky light to find as you wander about Portishead, but the coastal path reveals all.

The Groin Lighthouse, South Shields, Tyne and Wear

This wonderfully eccentric light was built by the
Newcastle Trinity House Board in 1880. By 1882 it was
casting its 21-kilometre (13-mile) beam out across the
mouth of the Tyne, and warning of enveloping fogs
with a bell behind the white railings that tolls every
five seconds. I have a thing about corrugated iron,
and obviously got overwrought by the sight of this
Wellsian Martian standing out on The Groin at South
Shields in white plimsolls. This is an exhilarating spot
on a kind day, with views across the river to
Tynemouth Castle and Priory.

right top
**A lighthouse with
personality, South
Shields**

right bottom
**The *City of Sunderland*
enters the Tyne**

opposite top
**Cast iron on the
Severn Estuary**

opposite bottom
**Structural nuts and
bolts at Blacknore**

Beachy Head Lighthouse, East Sussex

The South Downs sheer off abruptly at Beachy Head – and sometimes very suddenly as sections of chalk cliff fall onto the rocky shore. Building a lighthouse here was no mean feat, a cableway being constructed on the cliff top in order to lower 3,660 tons of Cornish granite to where the site was contained within a wave-resisting coffer dam. Sir Thomas Matthews, the Trinity House engineer-in-chief, superintended the massive undertaking in 1902. Although on the coastline stretching between Eastbourne and Seaford, Beachy Head (taking it's name from 'Beau Chef', beautiful headland) is one of our most inaccessible lighthouses. Walking here on the beach is a gruelling activity and very unadvisable owing to the tides, so the best bet is to take a pleasure boat from Eastbourne, or peek nervously over the cliff top. But don't go too near the edge unless you want to find yourself unexpectedly down on the rocks. And don't attempt to emulate Phil Daniel's airborne scooter ride in *Quadrophenia*.

Happisburgh Lighthouse, Norfolk

The Norfolk shore creeps ever nearer this 25.9-metre-(85-foot-) tall tower out in the fields, the result of dramatic coastal erosion. A true beacon of hope, this is perhaps the lighthouse of our imaginations, a 1790 tower that was originally one of a pair, warning of a treacherous stretch of coast. The lantern is 40.8 metres (134 feet) feet above sea level. It is also a landmark and seamark that was not only saved by the local community as a working light, but is also maintained entirely by volunteers. Happisburgh is the oldest lighthouse in East Anglia, standing out against the sky along with its companion, the tower of St Mary's Church in the village. Here, within earshot of the dull boom of waves, the graveyard enfolds the remains of those shipwrecked on this remote curve of Norfolk.

opposite
**Down on the shore,
Beachy Head Lighthouse**

below
**Out in the fields,
Happisburgh
Lighthouse**

Holborn Head Lighthouse, Scrabster, Highland

This is just about as far north as you can get on the British mainland. You will see the lighthouse on Holborn Head as you leave Scrabster on the ferry for Stromness on the Orkney Islands. In lighthouse parlance, it first 'exhibited' its light on Monday 1 September 1862. The Notice to Mariners stated: 'The light will be a dioptric holophotal flashing light. Showing a flash every 10 seconds, it will be seen as a white light towards the Pentland Firth and Thurso Bay and as a red light towards Scrabster roadstead.'

The engineers were members of the Scottish lighthouse family – David and Thomas Stevenson. Mr Stewart was the contractor, Mr James Scott the inspector. There is much surviving correspondence concerning the costs of building, the Board of Trade in Edinburgh being alarmed at an estimate of £3,900. The light became automated in 1988, finally closing altogether in August 2003.

Ardgour Lighthouse, Highland

Landmark buildings in Scotland often benefit greatly from having such dramatic backdrops. Driving down the A82 from Fort William alongside the shore of Loch Linnhe, a bend in the road suddenly reveals this scene where the loch squeezes through the Corran Narrows. A ferry waits to go over from Nether Lochaber to Ardgour, where this pretty lighthouse was built in 1860, again by the Stevensons.

A light became necessary here as shipping increased through the bottleneck with the expansion of the paper industry at Fort William. The light is still operational, flashing its red beacon every four seconds.

opposite
The Holborn Head lighthouse in the far north of Scotland in Scrabster

right
The ferry waits on a cold November morning to cross the Corran Narrows to Ardgour

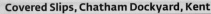

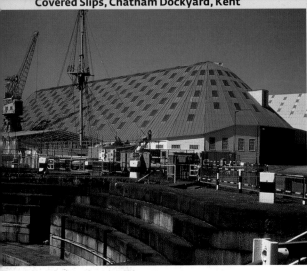

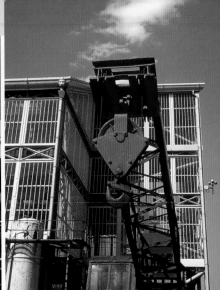

Slips were where wooden sailing ships were built and launched, undercover so that rot didn't set in prematurely. Here in Chatham Dockyard are a set of superbly nautical buildings, including the vast humpback No 3 slip, in itself like an upturned boat. Built in 1838, it was constructed in wood with the roofing material originally of tarred paper, which not surprisingly was replaced fairly quickly with zinc. In 1900 the slipway was abandoned and a mezzanine floor added inside to facilitate its conversion to a storehouse for ships' boats. No 7 slip has recently been restored, a vast glass-walled covered slipway designed in 1852 by Colonel GT Green RE. HMS *Ocelot* was launched here in 1962, in what still looks like an extremely modern structure with one of the earliest metal-trussed roofs. Shipbuilding in the No 7 slip ceased in 1966.

above left
The upturned boat-shaped No 3 slip, Chatham Dockyard

above right
Section of No 7 slip, Chatham Dockyard

Wells-next-the-Sea Lifeboat Station, Norfolk

The Wells Lifeboat Station on the North Norfolk coast is a sheep in wolf's clothing. When I first knew it, it was a collection of corrugated-iron barns with curved roofs, with a series of masts connected by wires acting as the communication system. And then one morning I walked down from the harbour to see this, a new lifeboat station with a pristine, and thoughtful, rendering of the original paint scheme of cream and maroon. Except it isn't really a replacement. Much of the original 1895 station is still inside; what you see on the exterior is a new suit of weatherproof clothes, a brilliant solution to the changing needs of the lifeboat service.

If the tide is in, then the D-class lifeboat is launched straight into the waves down the boat ramp on the north side. When it isn't, a Talus tractor with submersible tracks will tow the boat to launching sites on the beach, the furthest being two miles away – one of the longest of this type of beach launch in the UK.

below
On the beach: Wells-next-the-Sea's Lifeboat Station

Eastbourne Pier, East Sussex

If there's one name that keeps cropping up when it comes to piers, it's Eugenius Birch. Something of an engineering child prodigy, he put his skills to use in the burgeoning railway age. This took him to India, but on his return he concentrated on bridges and viaducts, just as their design principles were being recognised in marine construction. Birch saw the future, and it was the seaside pier. He got started with Margate, and over the next 30 years he was responsible for structures planted in the waves at 14 seaside resorts. Eastbourne Pier opened in 1872, 304.8 metres (1,000 feet) long with cast-iron screw piles supporting the 18.2-metre- (60-foot-) wide iron and wood frame. Once one gets past the burger franchises and a very worrying animatronic clown who swings about above the amusement arcade, the pier still shows off its architectural features well, including very fierce blue-painted lions on the lamp standard bases.

Clevedon Pier, North Somerset

Clevedon Pier is a remarkable survivor. Built on the Severn Estuary in 1868, it is a superb example of recycling, utilising as it does obsolete railway lines from the failed South Wales Railway. Designed by John Grover and Richard Ward, it paddled its spindly legs in the sea until it suffered the ignominy of losing a 61-metre (200-foot) section during an incredibly excessive load-bearing test in 1970. Clevedon nearly lost its pier, but local protest, grants and fundraising brought this unique and delicate pier back to life. It was meant to be. As restoration started, a stock of the same rails was discovered in some long-forgotten store. The pier perfectly suits this Somerset resort, with its Gothic and Italianate villas set amongst flowering shrubs and ilex trees.

opposite left
Lion lamp standard at Eastbourne

opposite right
Early evening in Eastbourne

above
End of the pier show, Clevedon

Wellington Pier, Great Yarmouth, Norfolk

As I write this, the pier of Weston-super-Mare in Somerset has just been destroyed by fire. These magnificent maritime fantasias have always been vulnerable, filigree cast-iron superstructures forever at the mercy of the waves and the odd stray ship, timber buildings just waiting for an overheated plug or a sheet of flame from a deep fryer in the kitchen. Brighton lost its West Pier, after decades of well-meaning action groups and local authorities wringing their hands without actually achieving anything. Watch Richard Attenborough's film *Oh! What a Lovely War* to see just how stunning it was in the late 1960s.

And then there was the Wellington Pier in Great Yarmouth, the place where for the first time I realised there was a comedian called Benny Hill, with his baby face smiling at me from a huge plywood cut-out. The original pier was designed in 1852 by Eastern Counties Railway engineer Peter Ashcroft, with the theatre pavilion added by JW Cockrill five decades later. Artistes called it 'the cow shed' because of the tarred roof, and hung fishing lines out of the dressing room windows. When I photographed it there was a very sad boarded-up feel that even The Grumbleweeds couldn't help.

Another comedian, Jim Davidson, was very fond of this pier and bought it in the 1990s, always saying that it must be the only pier in Britain that doesn't actually go out over the sea. His efforts, and an awful lot of his money, couldn't save it, and it was demolished. But, as if someone had waved yet another magic wand over this stretch of beach, a new structure is rising phoenix-like from the sand. Apparently it will be much like the original, only it won't be a theatre but a bowling alley.

Is there anything more visually satisfying, and at the same time instantly representative of the British seaside, than a row of beach huts? They have perhaps evolved in much the same way as we are supposed to have done, starting out in the sea and gradually crawling up to the top of the beach. For these gaily painted wooden huts and chalets have their beginnings in the bathing machines that our 19th-century ancestors used to hide in, prior to exhibiting their passion-killer swimming costumes and gingerly dipping delicate big toes in the water.

Modesty finally being overcome, the bathing machine lost its wheels and came to permanent rest at the beach head. Out came the paint pots, and individual identity was brought to the regimented rows. They are now much prized; if one comes up for sale it can be the price of a real house, even though you can't sleep in it. And if you want to optimistically put your name down to rent a chalet or beach hut, the waiting list's a coastline long. But don't let that put you off. There's no finer place to pump up a Lilo or a Primus stove.

opposite top
Old Hunstanton, Norfolk

opposite bottom
Wells-next-the-Sea, Norfolk

top right
Harwich, Essex

centre
Boscombe, Bournemouth

centre and bottom right
Fairbourne, Gwynedd

railways

Preparing for the off at
Wansford station on the
Nene Valley Railway in
Cambridgeshire

St Pancras Station, London

Much has been written about this station since its reopening as St Pancras International, a dramatic transformation from sad, soot-blackened train shed back to a light and airy iron-and-glass arched enclosure soaring over continental trains and champagne. Spruced up and with its iron bones freshly painted in the sky blue first applied in the 1870s. It is of course now a station of three thirds: George Gilbert Scott's Victorian Gothic-fronted former Midland Grand Hotel (where the first guests signed in on 5 May 1873), built in Nottingham red brick and Ancaster stone; William Henry Barlow's 1866–8 arched train shed, built on pillared vaults spaced out to take Burton beer barrels; and the new flat-roofed 2007 extension, built in the style of architecture's in-joke designer Mr Frank Juxtaposition – in other words, new meeting old in complete contrast without compromising the original. The western platform area has been opened up so that Barlow's undercroft iron pillars now stand sentinel to arcades of colour-supplement shops and chic coffee houses.

An interesting footnote to the building of the railway and station is a curious story about the exhumation and reburial of a portion of the dead buried in the old St Pancras churchyard, a corner of which lay in the path of the proposed tracks. Arthur Blomfield was the architect designated to carry out the excavations and, to ensure that everything was carried out with care and due reverence, he sent a 26-year-old Dorset man from his office to keep an eye on things. His name was Thomas Hardy, later to become one of our favourite authors and poets, who perhaps remembered his time here in his poem The Levelled Churchyard.

left and opposite top right
The restored original train shed, with roof supports repainted in the 1870s 'Barlow Blue', and the opened-up undercroft retail area

below
Sir George Gilbert Scott's Midland Grand Hotel for St Pancras station

left
Frank Juxtaposition at work between pillars (original) and safety barriers (new)

In many ways Settle station is the archetypal railway building. Local stone combines with decorative white bargeboarding on the gable ends, and everything else is freshly painted, in this case in the Midland Railway's crimson lake. Liberally applied to seats, barrel planters, doors, window frames and even the clock surround, this is the first taste of the 'Derby Gothic' stations to come as the Settle to Carlisle line sets off across 117 kilometres (73 miles) of difficult country, the highest mainline in Britain.

Traversing hill and dale in unpredictable weather, this was the Midland's 1870s alternative route to the north, still used by thundering coal trains crossing vast viaducts that stretch majestically over inhospitable hillsides sloping down to dark rushing streams. A true survivor, the Settle to Carlisle resisted countless attempts to close it, a fitting monument to those who simply would not see it all swept away on the whims and fancies of penpushers. And Settle station remains a defiant showpiece on the line, a superb railway modeller's template. On one of my visits the stationmaster was busy up a stepladder watering hanging baskets. It only needed a cat washing itself on a milk churn, eyeing up racing pigeons in their wicker baskets.

Denham Golf Club Station, Buckinghamshire

These once ubiquitous little corrugated iron buildings were supplied to the Great Western Railway (GWR) in kit form by Joseph Ash & Co of Birmingham, they went into service as lamp rooms, luggage stores and cycle sheds. But most of all they appeared on country platforms and trackside halts as passenger shelters. With their concave roofs they quickly earned the nickname 'pagodas', and 1912 examples are beautifully preserved here at Denham Golf Club station. The eponymous course is just under a mile to the west, and it's not difficult to conjure up plus-foured golfers arriving here and lighting up their Player's cigarettes in the dim recesses of the iron shelters.

below
Corrugated 'pagodas' at Denham Golf Club station

opposite
Gleneagles station, haunted by the ghosts of plus-foured golfers

Originally named Crieff Junction, Gleneagles station was rebuilt by the Caledonian Railway in 1919 in expectancy of the arrival of the grand hotel next door. The platforms are arched over by glazed canopies, something one would expect to find in a town or city station, and as I waited for snow-laden clouds to disperse I was all too aware of the ghosts of golfers and their caddies crowding out of the trains, the shouts of porters echoing up into the Ochil Hills. All is silent now, and instead of shooting brakes lined up outside, and liveried flunkies shouldering trunks and bags, the guest alighting here now for the hotel must pick up a wall phone that connects to the Gleneagles reception.

York Station

The uninspiring yellow brick entrance to York station does nothing to prepare the would-be train passenger for the splendours of the train shed. Built for the North Eastern Railway (NER), the design was executed by architect Thomas Prosser, under the supervision of the NER's Chief Engineer TE Harrison. Completed by William Peachey, it was opened in June 1877. Wrought-iron spans arc over the sharply curving platforms, finished off with graceful glazed end screens, and the spandrels of the supporting brackets still proudly bear the multicoloured heraldry of the NER. The station makes regular appearances in Andrew Martin's Jim Stringer Steam Detective novels (*The Lost Luggage Porter*, *Murder at Deviation Junction*) with his station police office situated between Platforms 4 and 13, a bay used solely for Hull-bound trains.

left
NER heraldry on the roof support spandrels

above
Evening light on York's platforms

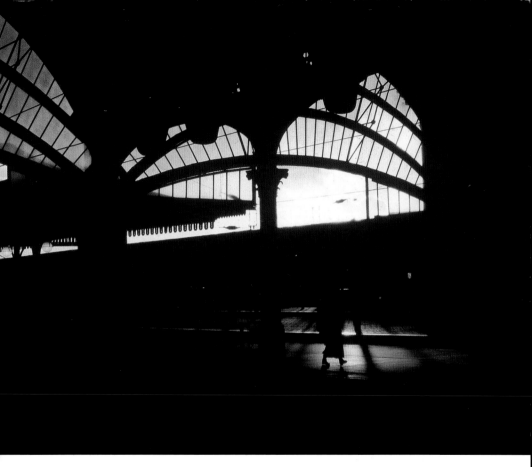

Folklore always gathers around dramatic structures. This is Brunel's 1-mile, 1,452-yard- (2.9-kilometre-) long Box Tunnel for his London to Bristol railway line between Corsham and Bath. They say that the rising sun shines through the tunnel only on 9 April, Brunel's birthday. In the 1840s this was the longest railway tunnel ever built, involving 4,000 men and 300 horses working around the clock by candlelight for five years. Where brick was used, they got through 30 million. After its opening in 1841 some passengers were very afraid of entering through either the eastern brick or the western Bath stone portals, so horses were kept for their convenience at either end to take them calmly over the top of the tunnel.

Kilsby Tunnel Ventilators, Northamptonshire

Two imposing brick castles stand each side of the A5 southeast of Rugby. They crown the shafts driven into the ground that were the first borings of Robert Stephenson's 1837 Kilsby Tunnel for the London & Birmingham Railway, at 2,194.5 metres (2,400 yards) the longest railway tunnel to be attempted at the time. The spoil from the resultant, often very dangerous, works can still be seen in the surrounding fields. Navvies would hold sometimes fatal sporting events where attempts were made to vault over the shaft openings before the castellated structures were built. Over a million bricks were used for each tower; folklore has it that the pub in Kilsby village was built with bricks finding their way off-site, and a contemporary stone model of one of the tunnel portals sits as an ornament in a local garden. What a sight it must have been in the steam railway age, to stand here and see intermittent billows of smoke rising up from so far below; and I wonder what the cows, those unconscious guardians of these doorless castles, made of it all?

opposite
The western portal of the Box Tunnel from the London to Bath Road

right
Railway buffs at Kilsby

Footbridges between station platforms, or as a convenient flyover for non-trainspotting pedestrians at level crossings, are amongst the most useful of bridges, but perhaps the least regarded. This example is a classic latticed iron prefabricated structure made for the Midland Railway and painted in their crimson lake and white colours. It crosses the Leicester to Peterborough line next to a signal box that provided Airfix model kits with their reference, and it is a measure of the durability and practicality of both these structures that they are conserved and maintained, rather than having to suffer the indignity of being replaced by something almost certainly of inferior quality and design.

Wilmcote Footbridge, Warwickshire

Wilmcote is a station on what was once the Great Western Railway's (GWR) new line across North Warwickshire, constructed in 1907. The thinking is that this evocative footbridge was moved here from another location, but it still proudly boasts the GWR's original cast-iron monogram and is finished in their dark and light stone colours. An iron notice nearby exhorts passengers to use the bridge in preference to making leaps of faith across the tracks.

opposite left
Detail of footbridge construction

opposite right
Freshly painted footbridge at the Oakham Level Crossing

above
Cast-iron rules at Wilmcote

right
GWR footbridge detail at Wilmcote in Warwickshire

Kemble is a Great Western Railway (GWR) station in the Tudor style and is dressed in warm Cotswold stone. The platform seats still have the distinctive GWR roundel cast as supports. At the north end is this superb iron water tank on stilts, built to serve a well sunk in 1903 and painted in the GWR's stone colours. Steam locomotives needed a ready supply of water for their tanks, but this leviathan also provided water for the GWR Swindon works 22.5 kilometres (14 miles) away, distributed by a pump house nearby. The tank also supplied the village of Kemble, and was originally fed by a spring discovered when the station was first built.

above
The GWR water tank at Kemble station

opposite left
Cast-iron piers of the demolished Blackfriars Bridge of 1864

opposite right
A Thameslink train passes behind the giant LCDR railway badge

LCDR Badge, Southwark, London

Walk south over Blackfriars Bridge and look down to your left. Down in the Thames can be seen a series of big pink cast-iron piers emerging impotently out of the water on stone bases, almost all that remains of Joseph Cubitt's railway bridge of 1864. They sit next to the extant railway bridge that takes Thameslink trains clattering out over the river and across the pies and olives of Borough Market. The spans may have gone, but on an abutment on the south side is this show stopper of a pylon bearing the cast-iron coat-of-arms of the London, Chatham & Dover Railway (LCDR).

This giant badge is a superb piece of public heraldry. The LCDR name encircles the arms of (clockwise from the top) Kent, Dover, Rochester and the City of London. And, as if all this wasn't enough, it is surmounted by Queen Victoria's 'V' and a flower border of red and white sunflowers. The 'Invicta' motto is taken from Kent's 'invincible' white horse, soon to be a landmark giant sculpture of Ebbsfleet.

military

A First World War
military ambulance at a
field hospital in English
Heritage's Festival of
History 2004

above
**Hadrian's Wall above
Housesteads Fort**

top right
**Landmark fir on
the wall above
Housesteads Fort**

bottom right
Foxgloves on the wall

Roman remains in Britain don't get much more impressive than this. 117.5 kilometres (73 miles) of stone wall stretching from Wallsend in the east to the shores of the Solway Firth, this was the most fortified border in the Empire. Constructed in AD 122 after a visit by Hadrian, this is one of four walls in the north made in an attempt to control Pictish hordes. So much has been written, and so much disagreed about this colossus of construction, it is difficult to put stylus to tablet without the clearing of the throat of an archaeologist. But it is generally agreed that there were once over 30 forts along the frontier, with around 80 milecastles and 160 turrets.

The Romans departed in the 5th century, and as soon as the echo of the last pair of sandals marching down the *Vallum Hadriani* was lost on the cold wind, the locals moved in and started removing the stones for monasteries, most notably for Lindisfarne. The stone proved irresistible to later builders, but thanks to a Newcastle town clerk, John Clayton, large sections were preserved in the 1830s. His interest started after a visit to Chesters Roman Fort, and he soon started buying up farmland which he managed himself, ploughing cash back into restoration work. One of the most famous paintings of life on the wall, by William Bell Scott and held at Wallington Hall near Morpeth, has Clayton's face given to an impressive centurion. But for the real thing, climb up westwards from Housesteads and look back along the wall towards the wooded ravine above the fort. It's like being at the very top of England.

These giant upturned sandcastles were built as defences against the very real probability of a Napoleonic invasion between 1805 and 1815, and despite Nelson's victory at Trafalgar. The Board of Ordnance built 164 Martello Towers around the most vulnerable shores on the southeast corner of England, from Aldeburgh in Suffolk to Seaford in East Sussex, leaving obvious gaps in the chain where high cliffs formed a natural defence. The most northerly, here in Aldeburgh, is also the largest, built on a quatrefoil plan and using around a million bricks to build walls up to 4 metres (13 feet) thick. The roof held a 24-pounder cannon on a rotating platform. The inspiration and name 'Martello' is a corruption derived from the impregnable Torre della Mortella fort in northern Corsica, where two Royal Navy ships were impressively fired upon in 1794.

Coalhouse Fort, East Tilbury, Essex

The reaches of the Thames on the approach to London were amongst the most heavily defended stretches of river in the country. Each bend provided an opportunity to build a fort, vantage points from which raking cannon-fire and gunfire could sweep hostile shipping. Here, out on the East Tilbury Marshes, is a massive granite fort begun in 1870 at Coalhouse Point. The curving walls were designed to deflect gunfire, and also to offer numerous placings for firing platforms in deeply embedded casements that in some cases were 7 metres (20 feet) thick. This was the era of advancement in iron-clad ships, so heavyweight artillery and ammunition was required in order to repel attacks from the water. Coalhouse Fort continued in use during the First World War, and naturally proved to be a very active anti-aircraft position in the Second.

Sound Mirrors, Greatstone-on-Sea, Kent

A precursor of radar as we know it today, these experiments in shaped concrete were built in the late 1920s in a not entirely unsuccessful attempt to predict the arrival of enemy aircraft to our shores. Now out on an island between gravel pits on the Dungeness peninsula, they can only be seen in detail on open days, but their indomitable shapes have intrigued visitors to this vast acreage of shingle since their incongruous arrival.

They work by the expedient of placing a microphone at the acoustical centre of the surfaces,

the sound of a potential raider being transmitted to a headphoned boffin hiding in a bunker. The 60.9-metre- (200-foot-) long near-vertical wall is one of only two in existence, the other being in Malta, but for me the most evocative of the three structures here is the 9.1-metre (30-foot) mirror that still retains its microphone stand. They were part of a plan to place sound mirrors in a sequence along the south coast, including a superb 6-metre (20-foot) example high on the more easily accessible Abbot's Cliff at Capel-le-

Ferne east of Folkestone. As was seen in an edition of the BBC's *Coast*, these science-fiction structures obviously did, and still do, work to a limited degree, but their application to modern warfare was quickly superseded by radar in 1932.

opposite top left
The three sound mirrors

opposite right
The 9.1-metre (30-foot) sound mirror

opposite bottom left
The 6-metre (20-foot) sound mirror on Abbot's Cliff near Folkestone

above
The 60.9-metre (200-foot) sound mirror on Denge Marsh

Airship Hangars, Cardington, Bedfordshire

These simply gigantic buildings have been arresting the attention ever since they were first built in the early 20th century at Cardington in Bedfordshire. The first of the two airship hangars was built in 1917, the second brought here in 1928 from Pulham St Mary in Norfolk. My father first pointed them out to me from a train as it left Bedford station; later he showed me little sepia snapshots he took here of the prodigious R101 airship just prior to its tragic demise in a muddy French field near Beauvais in 1930.

They are 247 metres (812 feet) long and 83.8 metres (275 feet) wide, and Nelson's Column would fit inside them – upright. The doors are opened by motors running on their own little railway track. To stand inside one is a strange experience, an enclosed world that seems too vast to produce even an echo, and on my visit the southern hangar housed a nine-storey office block and an airliner fuselage, both used to train firefighters. These awe-inspiring structures are well worth making a detour for, not only to see the site but also to visit Cardington church, where the tattered remains of the RAF ensign rescued from the wreckage of the R101 can be seen up on the south wall. The dead from this disaster are all buried in a communal grave, also in the village.

below
The twin Cardington Airship Hangars and the asliding entrance doors moving on their own railway track

RAF Hemswell, Lincolnshire

Ever since we've been able to master powered flight, we've needed somewhere to keep the 'plane. Portable canvas hangars were created by Julien Bessoneau in 1910, and they quickly became a Great War staple. Portability was the essence as the line of opposing fronts altered, and speed of manoeuvre was essential.

Something more substantial and permanent was required in the run-up to the Second World War, as airfields were rapidly built across the south and east, particularly here on the levels of Lincolnshire. There had been an airfield here at Hemswell during the First World War, but these Type C hangars were erected in the expansion programme and opened with the residence of 61 and 144 Squadrons in 1937. The Hampden bombers from Hemswell are credited with being the first Bomber Command aircraft to release their bombs over Germany. Aircraft no longer taxi out onto the tarmac, and the hangars have been variously put to use as grain stores and weekend marketplaces.

below
Out in remote Lincolnshire, east of Gainsborough, the Type C hangars at Hemswell

The Second World War saw a proliferation of airfields, and Lincolnshire in particular lost much agricultural land in the defence of the realm. Sturgate was one of the last airfields to be built in the war, too late to see operational service, but it did act from 1944 as a support base to the surrounding airfields, in particular RAF Scampton (now the home of the Red Arrows) and Hemswell. At the close of the war, Sturgate became a US Air Force base for training jet fighter pilots.

We are all familiar with the concept of the control tower, a glass eyrie at the top of a slim tower. But the wartime tower, usually an additional storey on a 'watch office', was a much simpler building – plain or rendered brick, metal windows and the tower often reached by an outside iron staircase. There was a time when I used to optimistically climb up into these wartime structures to see if there was still a Vargas pin-up calendar pinned to the back of the door – airbrushed distractions from more vital observances.

above
Deserted control tower at Sturgate Airfield

Cambridgeshire Pillboxes

It must have seemed as though England woke up one morning in 1940 to find the countryside suddenly littered with anti-tank barricades, vehicle traps and the ubiquitous pillbox. The threat of German invasion in 1940 resulted in 28,000 of these little concrete fortresses being placed in strategic locations – hidden in spinneys on the crests of fields, on the bends of rivers and at road junctions. All for a war that never came. And so, instead of heroic tales of rattling machine-gun fire raking across canals and cabbage fields, there must be countless tales of rehearsal, all-too-real manoeuvres or simply just rotas of guard duty that involved enamelled coffee pots and poaching in surrounding woods. These examples are out on the Cambridgeshire Fens: remote at the side of a road near Thorney, and on the bank of the old course of the River Nene near Benwick, just two of less than 6,000 still extant in the countryside.

above left
Pillbox on the River Nene at Copalder Corner on the B1093 near Benwick

above right
Pillbox on the B1443 between Newborough and Thorney near Powder Blue Farm

The Romney is a Nissen hut on steroids. The requirement for pre-manufactured buildings that could be easily transported and quickly erected on site became an urgent prerogative in the First World War in order to house troops and act as makeshift hospitals, stables and stores. The original semicircular huts were designed by Major Peter Nissen of the Royal Engineers in 1916, and one building could be fitted into a 3-ton army truck and erected by six men in around four hours. Their radial shape meant that bombs and shrapnel were more easily deflected.

The Romney hut was simply a larger version, 10.9 metres (36 feet) across the base with a 5.4-metre (18-foot) radius. The roof supports are hoops made up from four sections positioned at 2.4-metre (8-foot) intervals, making this example 29.3 metres (96 feet) long. An interesting footnote is that one of these particular Romney huts, now used as a stonemason's saw shed, is painted in the surplus army green paint intended for use during the 1956 Suez Crisis.

below
Romney Hut at Spanhoe Airfield, Northamptonshire

opposite
Romney Hut at Spanhoe used as a saw shed

Around here is classic Cheshire countryside. Cattle slowly grazing over quiet pastures, woods of oak and ash and winding tree-shaded lanes. So it really does come as a jaw-dropping surprise to drive round a bend and see this gigantic skeletal construction dominating the landscape. This is Jodrell Bank, the 76-metre (250-foot) radio telescope renamed in 1987 the Lovell Telescope after its creator Sir Bernard Lovell. The prodigious white dish really does look as if it's bending an ear to the far sides of universes, straining to catch the slightest glimmer of activity in other worlds. I've put it in the military chapter for want of a more appropriate place in this book, but even if it's not used to eavesdrop on unfriendly bombers taking off and marching jackboots, it will

certainly be in the forefront of noticing the approach of alien spacecraft.

In 1945 Dr Lovell, as he then was, returned to the University of Manchester after his war work in radar. He wanted to continue his pre-war research into cosmic rays, those energetic particles flying towards us from space, but radio interference in the city led to his early apparatus being set up at the University's Botanical Station at Jodrell Bank, 32 kilometres (20 miles) away. No cosmic rays were noticed by the first telescope, but radio waves from the Andromeda Galaxy were detected by a collection of scaffolding poles and a bowl the size of the field it was in. The Mark 1 version of the telescope as we see it today began trials in 1957, and within months was the first

to follow the flight path of the Soviet Union's Sputnik 1 satellite. Now, this cat's cradle of a telescope not only has a resolution as high as the Hubble telescope, it has acted for 50 years as a thought-provoking inspiration to children who took up science as a career. So of course the Government want to close it down to save money, probably in order to divert cash into the science-free Olympic Black Hole. Sign up for its survival today.

left
Jodrell Bank cat's cradle

below
Cheshire guardians

opposite
Dawn on Earth

leisure

Torn poster scraps at the
Wellington Pier, Great
Yarmouth, Norfolk

The People's Palace on Glasgow Green is an exhibition hall and glasshouse opened by the Earl of Rosebery in 1898. Situated to the east of the great city, this was an opportunity for the working classes of Glasgow (who could never even dream of having gardens, let alone greenhouses) to enjoy the pleasures that only big green plants thrusting up into the 18.2-metre- (60-foot-) high glass roof space can give. A very welcome change from their grinding existences in tenements and factories.

It was constructed for the Glasgow Corporation by Boyd & Son of Paisley, a large winter garden formed from cast-iron pillars supporting latticed arch girders. There are not many surviving glass spaces on this scale, and I can thoroughly recommend it for a mug of hot chocolate on a wintry but sunny morning, seeing the clouds scud over the towers and spires of Glasgow city centre away across the greensward.

opposite
The interior of the glasshouse at the People's Palace

above
The glasshouse from Glasgow Green

Grand Hotel, Scarborough, North Yorkshire

Can there be a more iconic Victorian seaside hotel than this? The Grand Hotel has seen grander days, but although cigar-chuffing Bradford millionaires no longer lever themselves out of limousines, Cuthbert Brodrick's 1867 monolith still dominates the Scarborough seafront. The owners simply had to make the hotel an ultimate symbol of prosperity, and it quickly gained its own architectural mythology. One room for every day of the year, and the idea that the ground plan makes a 'V' for Victoria, although the latter perhaps owes more to the awkward cliff-top site.

Once I'd battled my way through the holidaymakers disgorging from coaches, I was given the key to one of the dormer-windowed attic rooms. The views of Scarborough Castle and the harbour are magnificent, the view straight down vertiginous. Coming down for breakfast, one is very tempted to do a Fred Astaire impression on the grand staircase. But one puzzle still remains. Is it part of the building's mythology that the three corner turrets now look like Dr Who aliens peeping over the parapets?

right
**Early morning
from the beach**

opposite
**Late evening from the
south**

Angel of the North, Gateshead

They say that 33 million people see the *Angel of the North* every year. That's because apart from those gathering at the feet of Britain's largest sculpture on Low Fell above Gateshead, it can also be seen from both the A1 and the east-coast railway line. Designed by Antony Gormley, whose own body shape informs both this and many of his other sculptures, the *Angel* tons of concrete above a disused coalmine. It has become a trademark for the North East, and quite rightly is one of the most popular pieces of public art in the country, although there was initially some vociferous opposition. After the *Angel* landed in 1998 it quickly became a symbol for regeneration and for the acceptance of such powerful expressions of public

is 20.1 metres (66 feet) high, and the width of the outstretched wings is longer than the height of the Statue of Liberty.

The 220-ton structure is made from weathering steelwork that has to withstand winds of over 160 kilometres (100 miles) per hour, and is rooted in 661 art, and at the time of writing the full-size maquette used in the creation of the sculpture was sold at auction for £2 million.

Willow Man, Bridgwater, Somerset

All too often our motorways and major roads can be bereft of anything really arresting to mark our passages. There are of course exceptions; I always look out for the neo-Norman water tower at Middleton Stoney on a particularly bland stretch of the M40 north of Oxford, and I only really feel I'm in the West Country when I look down on the magnificent Clevedon Waterworks on the M5 south of Bristol. And then of course, just a little further down the same motorway, this amazing eyecatcher strides through the meadows near Bridgwater.

This is *Willow Man*, Somerset's bucolic answer to the *Angel of the North*. He is indeed made from willow, the crop that so typifies the Somerset Levels that stretch out to the horizon here, and was sculpted by Serena de la Hey. The first *Willow Man* on the site was burned down in May 2001, doubtless in imitation of the final scene in the film *The Wicker Man* but with, as far as I remember, no fresh-faced copper screaming inside. This second incarnation, constructed immediately after the destruction of the first, has an outer skin of willow interwoven over a steel skeleton and reinforced with steel thread.

opposite
North East Icon. *The Angel of the North* on Low Fell in Gateshead

right
The *Willow Man* striding through the fields at the side of the M5 in Somerset

Another Place, Crosby, Lancashire

One hundred cast-iron life-size figures paddle and sunbathe along the shore at Crosby, just north of Liverpool. Stretching for nearly two miles along the beach, and over 900 metres (1,000 yards) out to sea, *Another Place* is public sculpture at its most imaginative and exciting. As I walked from the car park towards the dunes, I suddenly had the thought that I was in the wrong place. On asking a returning couple for reassurance they said yes, but be quick, the tide's coming in very fast. This I hadn't expected, that a fair proportion of these men actually get submerged under the Crosby Channel.

Those who know and admire Antony Gormley's work will immediately recognise these self-referenced castings, down-to-earth (and sea) follow-ups to his really big idea of the *Angel of the North*. Each weighs in at a hefty 650 kilos, and they are positioned to varying degrees of depth. All look out expectantly at the horizon. Cuxhaven in Germany, Stavanger in Norway and De Panne in Belgium have all welcomed these rust-tanned iron men staring out at their respective seascapes, and they were scheduled to move out across this same sea to New York. But we liked them too much and so got their deportation papers withdrawn. They're here to stay.

right
Full-frontal iron

opposite
Beach snaps of Antony Gormley's *Another Place*

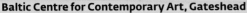

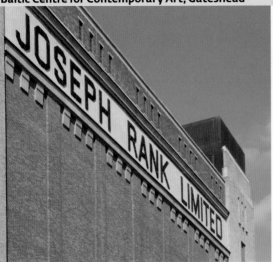

Sometimes developers get accused, rightly or wrongly, of a practice that goes under the name of facade-ism. This is where, in order to placate the last-ditch attempts by conservationists or indeed as a reasonable compromise, the facades of old buildings are kept standing as stage fronts for new replacements that need a totally different interior infrastructure. In most cases this practice is, I think, perfectly acceptable if it means that the look of a well-loved streetscape or environment is preserved. At the very least it shows some recognition of what has informed an area in the past, sadly lacking in much of what we have to put up with in new building.

Here on the quayside at Gateshead is a particularly successful example. The milling firm of J Arthur Rank built the Baltic Flour Mills in 1950, including a simply enormous silo for the storage and cleaning of wheat before milling. A fire in 1982 finally put paid to the mills, but the silo survived subsequent demolition of the mills to be reborn as Baltic, a free art gallery that has added much to the regeneration of Gateshead. The conversion, designed by Ellis Williams Architects and completed in 2002, retained the north and south elevations, still proudly displaying the original lettering.

The Sage, Gateshead

opposite
**Flour into art –
Baltic in Gateshead**

left and below
**Looks good, sounds good
– The Sage in Gateshead**

In complete, but very successful, contrast to the Baltic is The Sage. This sinuously curved glass and stainless-steel concert hall, started in 1997 and completed in 2004, sits on the same Gateshead quayside, a masterful building by Foster & Partners in conjunction with structural engineers Mott Macdonald and the appropriately named Arup Acoustics. The glass shell, echoing the other curves of the Tyne bridges, encases a more traditional 'shoebox' performance space where the acoustics can be finely adjusted with moveable screens. Orchestras occupy a parabolic dish that acts as a further enhancer to the quality of the sound.

To drop down now onto the Gateshead waterfront is to experience a powerful example of 21st-century regeneration. Not the wholesale destruction of the past, but a very happy combination of Tyneside's traditional structures with new and exciting ideas that are already perfectly at home here. Ample evidence is provided by the stunning views from the walkway inside The Sage.

Alexandra Palace, Wood Green, London

Ally Pally. Just the nickname tells of the affection this structure is held in by Londoners. After years of seeing it from trains approaching Kings Cross (one of those landmarks you look out for so that you know when to fold up your newspaper), I finally made the ascent one hot summer morning, and found the details as fascinating as the awesome exhibition halls themselves. This was the northern counterpart to the Crystal Palace that once crowned the heights of Sydenham to the south, burnt down in 1936. As if in some fiery portent, this building spectacularly burst into flames just 16 days after opening in 1873.

The designers and engineers for the extant buildings were Alfred Meeson and John Johnson, and their creation finally came to fruition in 1875. A railway also arrived at the top of the hill at a now-closed terminus on the north side. And what did they get up to on this airy hillside with its fabulous views of the capital? The 1881 Daily Programme for the August Bank Holiday promised Dr Holden, Little Salvini, 'Trial by Jury', Clown Cricketers, Circus, Drums and Fifes, Giant Punch & Judy, Shadow Pantomime and, just for good measure, the Destruction of the Spanish Armada.

Later of course the name Alexandra Palace became inextricably linked with the pioneering early days of the BBC. The incongruous 61-metre- (200-foot-) high mast on the southeast corner reminds us that the world's first regular 'high-definition' television service was transmitted from here on 2 November 1936,

ten-inch blue screens flickering into life in a handful of wealthy homes within a 40-kilometre (25-mile) radius of the hill. Exciting times, and on my hot visit (relieved by an ice-cold lager amongst the ferns) I experienced that same sense of expectancy that Victorians, Edwardians and every Londoner since must have felt on arriving at this hilltop palace for the people.

opposite
Alexandra Palace on a North London hilltop, from the south

below right
Detail of lamp standard

below left
The domed Palm Court

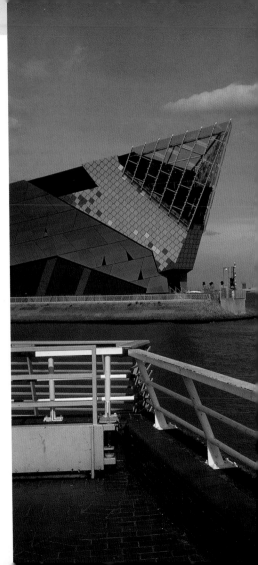

The Deep, Hull, East Riding of Yorkshire

Sir Terry Farrell obviously either had a close encounter with a shark, or had looked at re-runs of the film *Jaws*, when his architectural practice came up with the design for The Deep, the world's only 'submarium' – a new name for a new concept in aquaria. If sharks are your thing, then The Deep will introduce you to 40 of them, plus 3,500 other fish that presumably eye them nervously from adjoining tanks.

This is one of the more imaginative Millennium projects, its snout rearing up over Sammy's Point on the Humber Estuary. Inside, the centrepiece is the 2.5-million-litre (550,000-gallon) aquarium tank, where an underwater lift and viewing gallery bring you face to fin with fabulous creatures. And if all this isn't enough, you can book the stunning surroundings for business conferences and weddings, bringing perhaps a new slant to the phrase 'shark-infested waters'.

right
Sir Terry Farrell's shark's nose juts out into the Humber

opposite
Decimus Burton's Kew Gardens skyline and staircase to palm heaven

Palm House, Kew Gardens, London

Wandering about across the lawns and under the trees of Kew Gardens, one's eye, and indeed imagination, is immediately caught by the sensual, shimmering glass curves of the Palm House, a glorious bubble rising almost organically up out of the fertile soil. This classic greenhouse was planted here in 1844–8, and there is still a long-running debate as to who should take credit for its design. The latest consensus is that Decimus Burton was responsible for the look of it, at least of the central section, and Richard Turner for the layout and engineering of the wrought-iron framework. Whoever did what, whatever compromises were made, their collaboration has resulted in something very special indeed.

This is an ultimate expression of 'outside inside', a seductive tropical climate encased in glass. White-painted iron staircases spiral up amongst the fronds and leaves stretching up towards a sky that is always just out of reach. All accompanied by a soundtrack of hissing hoses and the gentle pattering of water droplets amongst the greenery. A little further away is Burton's Temperate House, and although he had much more freedom here and expressed it with a built-in ventilation system and ornamental urns and pinnacles, it's the Palm House that is the more impressive innovation of the mid-Victorian age.

The London Eye

'Enjoy a glass of Laurent-Perrier champagne served by your host while you take in amazing views of the capital'. This is how the London Eye introduces you to this sky-scraping big wheel. Now as much a part of the London skyscape as the Big Ben clock tower across the river, these glass capsules first revolved fee-paying passengers up for a pigeon's-eye view of the city in March 2000. Book your 'flight' early – over 3.5 million passengers ascend above County Hall every year.

When I first saw it, the London Eye was lying on the Thames, face down on the water by Westminster Bridge. Seeing it being constructed, it seemed impossible that it would rise up to be as tall as it is, not unlike the feeling you get when you see just the foundations of a new home and think 'It can't possibly be this small'. Well, the London Eye more than rose to the occasion. The apple of the eye of husband-and-wife architects David Marks and Julia Barfield, the wheel is 135 metres (442 feet) high, takes 30 minutes to rotate and gives views of 40 kilometres (25 miles) in every direction – which means you should be able to see Basildon, should you be so inclined.

top right
Details of capsules

top and centre
The London Eye from Westminster Bridge

opposite
Towering centrepiece of countless Lancashire coast holidays

Blackpool Tower, Lancashire

Although very obviously highly influenced by the Eiffel Tower in Paris, Blackpool Tower was not designed by Monsieur Eiffel. And unlike its Parisian relation it is not freestanding but perched on the Circus building underneath. Blackpool mayor John Bickerstaffe had the idea after his visit to Paris's Exposition Universelle in 1889, and put £2,000 of his own money into the project, designed by Lancashire architects James Maxwell and Charles Tuke. By the time it was opened in 1894 the tower and supporting buildings had cost around £290,000 and both architects were dead.

If ever one had to choose just one instantly memorable seaside resort landmark, this would surely be it. At 158 metres (518 feet 9 inches) high, it can apparently be seen from as far away as Barrow-in-Furness and Manchester, and is designed to fall into the sea if it collapses. Three years after the opening the top caught fire (flames seen 80 kilometres [50 miles] away) and also in the early days its light was once mistaken for a lighthouse by a ship early into its passage from Liverpool to Florida. The wreck can still be seen at low tide at Bispham. Everyone from Paderewski to Arthur Askey has performed here, and of course it's lit up like a Christmas tree as part of the Blackpool illuminations.

Midland Hotel, Morecambe, Lancashire

Morecambe Bay comes an expansive airy surprise after the constrictions and bottlenecks of its neighbour Lancaster. The North Western Railway (NWR) built a terminus station here in Morecambe with an accompanying hotel, but after their amalgamation into the London, Midland & Scottish Railway (LMS) it was replaced by the classic Art Deco-style Midland Hotel in 1933. Designed by Oliver Hill, it had all the ultra-fashionable details of its age: flat roofs, white stucco rendering, seahorse motifs, concrete balconies and a curved glass-walled tearoom. Contemporary 'in' designers travelled up here to decorate the interior walls, including Eric Gill and Eric Ravilious with his wife Tirzah.

During the Second World War the Midland was requisitioned as a military hospital, being given back to the LMS in 1946. The hotel went into gradual decline, and by the late 1980s was rapidly decaying. Eventually rainwater seeped in and removed the Ravilious mural as this Grade 2-listed building became a sad, neglected wreck. Thank goodness for Urban Splash, the Manchester developers, who spent proper money in restoring it to its former glory and reopened it. Not as an Art Deco pastiche, but as a very stylish new breed of seaside hotel that takes the 1930s features only as a starting point. The architects were Union North, the structural repairs undertaken by Whitby Bird and completed in 2008.

opposite
Seaside style – the Midland Hotel on Morecambe's seafront

above
A stylish 1930s-inspired bar that replaces the Midland Hotel tearoom

I wonder what Birmingham thought of this when the scaffolding was removed. So used to the harsh brutal concrete that turned the city centre into Motopolis in the 1960s, these seductive curves may just have brought a sigh of relief. The fact that the building is a department store rather than a windowless office must have been another surprise. The basic shell is, in fact, still concrete (albeit sprayed blue), but with around 15,000 aluminium discs attached to its skin like the scales of some ambitious reptile.

Future Systems, who gave us the Aardman Animations mouth-shaped Lords Cricket Ground Media Centre, designed the store for Selfridges in 2001–3, to a brief that specified that the interior should be completely divorced from the exterior. The result is mind-boggling, and cartoonists quickly turned it into an instant icon that of course had typical Brummie-humoured labels attached to it – The Blob and Digbeth Dalek being just two. Apparently from the air it looks like a gigantic sofa.

opposite
How to disguise a department store

right
Shopkeeper's sales promotion in the heart of Birmingham

Maxim's Captive Flying Machine, Blackpool

Sir Hiram Maxim was a serial inventor. To his name has been attached everything from mousetraps to light bulbs, but it's for the first portable machine gun that he will be remembered most. Maxim became profoundly deaf, doubtless from spending his working hours setting off explosions, but he also had an abiding passion for powered flight. To this end he needed to invent something that would bring him the streams of cash necessary, and so the Captive Flying Machine was born. Based on the rig he devised to test his aeroplanes, the fairground ride consisted of a large spinning frame from which cars were suspended. As the speed of the ride quickened, so the cars flew outwards. The first machine spun round at the 1904 Earls Court Exhibition; subsequently they were erected at the Crystal Palace in Sydenham and at Southport, but it's at Blackpool's Pleasure Beach that the only surviving Flying Machine still works for its living. The cars are now bland wingless aircraft fuselages, but the original machinery still pounds away underneath. Extinguish all cigarettes and fasten your seatbelts please.

left
Sole survivor – Sir Hiram Maxim's money-spinner at Blackpool's Pleasure Beach

How could anybody possibly not stop and photograph this? Just around the corner from Farringdon station, an exceptionally pink set of shapes drops into the Benjamin Street Gardens in Clerkenwell like a party blancmange behind a hedge. Underneath it all is a park keeper's shed, temporarily transformed by students (working at architects Wilkinson Eyre) as their contribution to the 2008 London Festival of Architecture. Islington Council's Greenspace team hope that it will kick off more public art in Clerkenwell, and sadly it's more than likely that this eye-scorching showstopper will have been dismantled by the time that you read this. But I think it's a very useful pointer to the future, that there is an up-and-coming generation that is prepared to think outside the box whatever colour it's painted; a very optimistic reminder that Britain can still delight us with the unexpected.

above
Anything But Grey, an experimental structure in the heart of Clerkenwell

First and foremost I must thank Mark Whitby at Ramboll Whitbybird for sponsoring this book, and for his unstinting support and good humour. Misha Anikst, Lucy Bland, Simon Bland, Boots Nottingham, , Helen Castle, Teresa Cox, Rupert Farnsworth, Abigail Grater, Richard & Jane Gregory, Jane Joyce, Owen Leyshon at the Romney Marsh Countryside Project, Lilian Sampson, Margaret Shepherd, Lorna Skinner, Ashley Smart at the Papplewick Pumping Station, David Stanhope, Amie Tibble, Philip Wilkinson, Yorkshire Waterways Museum.

opposite
Coal store at Papplewick Pumping Station, Nottinghamshire

Buildings of England Series, Penguin Books; *Shell County Guides*, Faber & Faber; Ian Nairn, *Nairn's London*, Penguin Books, 1966; Eric de Maré, *Your Book of Bridges*, Faber & Faber, 1963; Simon Bradley, *St Pancras Station*, Profile Books, 2007; Gordon Biddle, *Britain's Historic Railway Buildings*, Oxford University Press, 2003; Jack Simmons & Gordon Biddle (eds), *The Oxford Companion to British Railway History*, Oxford University Press, 1997; Peter Ashley, *Bridging the Gap*, Everyman & English Heritage, 2001; Peter Ashley, *Guiding Lights*, Everyman & English Heritage, 2001; Peter Ashley, *Railtrack: The Architectural Heritage*, Railtrack, 1999; Suzanne Beedell, *Windmills*, David & Charles, 1975; John Hix, *The Glasshouse*, Phaidon, 1996; WG Chapman, *Track Topics*, Great Western Railway, 1935; Chris Leigh, *GWR Country Stations* (2 vols), Ian Allan, 1981 & 1984; Philip Wilkinson & Peter Ashley, *The English Buildings Book*, English Heritage, 2006; Cyril Bainbridge, *Pavilions On The Sea*, Robert Hale, 1986; Anthony Murray, *The Forth Railway Bridge*, Mainstream, 1983; LTC Rolt, *Isambard Kingdom Brunel*, Longmans, Green, 1957.

List of structures

Index of architects, engineers, artists and builders

following page
**Detail of Newport Bridge,
Middlesbrough**

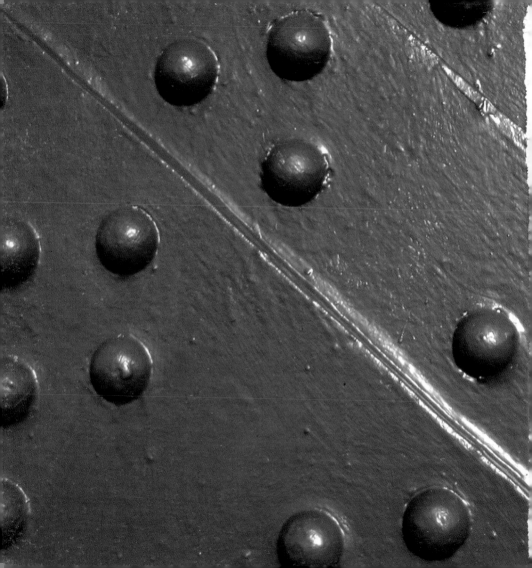